DEPOLITICIZING DEVELOPMENT

DEPOLITICIZING DEVELOPMENT

THE WORLD BANK AND SOCIAL CAPITAL

John Harriss

Anthem Press

This edition first published by Anthem Press 2002

Anthem Press is an imprint of
Wimbledon Publishing Company
PO Box 9779, London SW19 7QA

© 2001, LeftWord Books

British Library Cataloguing in Publication
Data available

Library of Congress Cataloguing in Publication Data
A catalogue record has been applied for

ISBN 1 84331 048 1 (hbk)
ISBN 1 84331 049 X (pbk)

Printed by Bell & Bain Ltd., Glasgow

1 3 5 7 9 10 8 6 4 2

Contents

Acknowledgements

I am very grateful to Sudhanva Deshpande of LeftWord Books, and V K Ramachandran and Prabhat Patnaik in India, and to James Putzel and Peter Loizos of the London School of Economics, for a judicious mixture of encouragement and of criticism on earlier drafts of this book; though I also want to exonerate them from any responsibility for its final content. I am further indebted to Professor Ben Fine of the School of Oriental and African Studies for allowing me to read and to make use of the text of his important book *Social Capital versus Social Theory: Political Economy and Social Science at the Turn of the Millennium* (London and New York: Routledge, 2001) in advance of its publication. Warm thanks, too, for various gifts of encouragement and friendship to Tony Barnett and Ben Rogaly at the University of East Anglia, to Stuart Corbridge at the LSE, and to Tom Penn at Anthem. Last, not least, I want to thank my family, especially my wife Gundi and my daughter Eli, for guaranteeing that 'social capital' which is most meaningful to me.

1

Introduction

The 'Missing Link' and the 'Anti-Politics Machine'

According to these arguments the cause of the weakness of development in parts of the Third World is 'lack of social capital'. But if the absence of civic capacity is the by-product of politics, state-building and social structure then the causes of the malaise (of development) are more likely to be structural. Then policy-makers who attack the lack of social capital would be attacking the symptoms and not the causes of the problem.
after Sidney Tarrow[1]

This book is about the prevailing discourse on 'development' emanating principally from the World Bank at the turn of the twentieth century, and the (mainly American) social science which supports it. Specifically, it is about an idea that was virtually unheard of outside a small circle of academic social scientists until about five years ago, but which now – in spite of, or perhaps because of the fact that there is still a great deal of confusion surrounding it – informs public policy very extensively. Ideas that can be interpreted in different ways (and may therefore become confused) are sometimes particularly powerful in 'policy-making' because they provide a spacious kind of hanger on which those of different persuasions are able to hang their coats. By now this particular idea has merited a reference in a presidential State of the Union address in the USA, and has been the subject of a great many symposia at prestigious academic gatherings. It was celebrated in India in May and June 2000 by the columnist Swaminathan S Anklesaria Aiyar in *The Sunday Times of India*, who found in it inspiration for the advocacy of 'caste-based development'. The idea is that of 'social capital', which is defined in a book on government in Italy by Robert Putnam, the Harvard professor who is responsible more than any other for its extraordinary, meteoric rise, as 'trust, norms and networks, that can improve the efficiency of society by facilitating coordinated actions'.[2] Put very simply, it refers to the familiar, everyday notion that 'It's not what you know [that counts] – it's who you know!'[3] Yet it has come to be described by one World Bank expert as 'the 'missing link' in development.[4]

This book asks why it is that such an apparently commonplace idea should have been elaborated – and made complicated and mystifying – in the way that it has been, and explores the purposes that are served by social capital. In the end the book aims to show how the work of often very clever and well-intentioned social scientists derives from and contributes to an hegemonic social science that systematically obscures power, class and politics. 'Social capital' and the closely related idea of 'trust', the ideas and activities around 'civil society' (held to be the sphere of association, outside the state, in which people freely participate), 'participation' and non-governmental organizations have – the book argues – come to constitute new weapons in the armoury of the 'anti-politics machine' that is constituted by the practices of 'international development'.[5] These are clever ideas which suit the interests of global capitalism (or in other words, present-day, US-centred imperialism) because they represent problems that are rooted in differences of power and in class relations as purely technical matters that can be resolved outside the political arena. They are directed in particular, therefore, against movements of the political left for progressive socio-political and economic change, which do identify the roots of poverty and social deprivation in class differences. Hence the title of this book. This introductory chapter sketches the idea of social capital as the 'missing link', and outlines the argument of the book as a whole.

Why the 'missing link'?

Organization is an asset

The fact that the idea of 'social capital' should have been invented and reinvented several times since 1916 – the date of the first recorded 'sighting' in the literature – probably shows that it has an intuitive appeal. This is because 'capital' itself is popularly understood to mean 'assets' or 'resources', which are of value in producing things. It is but a short step, then, to recognizing that social relationships themselves constitute resources. Marx (though of course he did not envisage 'capital' as 'stuff used to produce things',[6] but rather as a social relation) placed great emphasis on the 'resource' that is created by the organization of large numbers of people. For him an important part of the dialectics of capitalism lies in the fact that the development of capitalism is inseparable from the making of the working class which, as it becomes organized, has the means to change the social relations of production. Among the classical sociologists Emile Durkheim also recognized that social relationships constitute resources: the productivity of industrial society rests on a complex division of labour in which relationships of complementarity bind people together.

What makes organization possible? Is it 'social capital'?

But the idea of 'social capital' refers rather to conditions that make possible such organization of large numbers of people in pursuit of collective projects. It may be derived more specifically from the ideas of the philosophers of the Scottish Enlightenment who, reflecting upon what was happening in the industrializing, urbanizing world of their own time in the later eighteenth century, drew attention to the new significance of friendship. Their point was noted by the anthropologist Keith Hart in research on the Frafra people in Ghana in the 1960s.[7] Studying Frafra migrants in Accra, Hart found that they seemed in many ways to be stuck between the worlds of 'status', in which people can be relied upon to act in particular ways because they (mainly) follow the rules which are associated with ascribed social roles (depending, for example, upon their positions in the tribe), and of 'contract', when others can be relied upon to act in determined ways because of legal sanctions on their actions. Frafra migrants no longer lived in the world of status but neither did they yet live in the world of contract. In these circumstances, Hart showed, much depended upon ties of friendship. Having a network of friends, in the context he described, clearly represented an important asset. The case shows both that these kinds of networks are partly built upon, and serve to reinforce, trust between people, and the strong likelihood of reciprocity in the relationships between them. In these sorts of networks people can be fairly confident that others will reciprocate favours that are done to them, perhaps because membership in the group is an essential part of their identities, and certainly because they have a material interest in being able to go on relying on others for support and assistance. Hart might well have used the term 'social capital' – though he did not – to describe these resources (of trust and reciprocity) that arise in the context of networks of friendship among the migrants. This, in essence, is what the idea of 'social capital' means.[8] Where there is trust between people, and they can count on others reciprocating favours of any kind, then organization for different purposes is made easier. Of course large numbers of people can be organized through hierarchical structures of command and control, but all organizations work better the less they have to depend upon 'sticks'. Not for nothing is the slogan of the Mitsubishi automotive company 'Harmonious Discipline'.

Theorizing social capital

The idea of social capital was theorized in the 1980s by two writers of very different theoretical persuasions. The first was the French cultural theorist Pierre Bourdieu, a scholar who has shown persistent solidarity in his own life with working people and whose central interest has been in the ways in which social classes are reproduced especially through the constructions of meanings. In the course of his investigations he came up with the idea that 'connections' play a part in the reproduction of classes, and he pointed out that investment, for example, in membership of a prestigious club builds a sort of social capital which might be converted into economic capital. The 'possession' of particular durable social relationships, in other words, may provide for differential access to resources. In this view, 'social capital' is certainly not an attribute of 'society' as a whole, but it is an aspect of the differentiation of classes. Social capital, in this view, is really an instrument of power.[9]

Significantly, as I shall explain later, Bourdieu's contribution to the development of the notion of social capital has come to be very largely ignored. Attention has instead focused on the work of an

American sociologist, the late James S Coleman, who was a 'rational choice' theorist. He believed, in other words, that one can best build up social theory from a model of individual behaviour – the axiom that individuals seek to maximize the realization of their interests. Such a sociology tends to skate around the problem of how 'interests' are defined. Can they indeed be defined outside of specific social and cultural, and therefore historical, contexts? It is nevertheless a style of sociology that is attractive to neo-classical economists, those who rule the roost in that most powerful of social science research organizations, the World Bank, who work with the same basic model of human behaviour. Coleman argued that social capital 'inheres in the structure of relations between persons and among persons', and that it facilitates actions of the persons who are connected by 'the structure of relations'. Using a number of examples – such as that of traders in a Cairo market who share information about customers – he shows how the reciprocity and trust which may be an aspect of social relations are of value because they help to reduce many of the costs of transacting, through the communication of information and the kinds of insurance that are created in social networks (in which people recognize some obligations to help each other). In this account, although it is suggested that 'social capital' can have the characteristics of a public good, its fungibility is acknowledged to be constrained, and its 'value' is obviously context-specific.

Social capital becomes the 'missing link'

Bourdieu and Coleman between them, in their different ways, elaborate upon the common-sense argument which, I think, can be derived from an ethnography like that of Hart's on the Frafra. But if these two writers might be described as 'the philosophers of social capital', Robert Putnam has been the High Priest who has both transformed the idea in subtle ways and been responsible for winning masses of converts, convincing them that in social capital they have a concept that will help to solve many problems and change the world.

Putnam studied regional governments in Italy for more than twenty years from 1970 and sought to explain their strikingly contrasting performances. The upshot of his work was to 'demonstrate' statistically that both variations in government performance, and levels of socio-economic development in different parts of the country, are most strongly explained by a factor that he labels 'civic engagement', measured in terms of the extent and type of political participation, newspaper readership, and density of voluntary associations of different kinds (including choirs and sports teams, and groups like bird-watching clubs – in other words, organizations without specific political purposes). Later (for the idea of social capital evidently came as an afterthought in his work) 'civic engagement' is also described as 'social capital'. Contrary to both Bourdieu's and Coleman's conceptualizations, it has now become a property of a whole society. There is a confessed circularity in Putnam's argument, and it seems that higher levels of civic involvement give rise to 'social capital' which in turn makes possible more civic involvement (or 'civic engagement'). According to his analysis, north central Italy has lots of social capital dating back to the city republics of the Middle Ages, and because of this now has both better government and higher levels of economic development. The Italian South, on the other hand, has been locked into a negative set of social institutions for about as long a period. Interestingly Putnam locates the bases of these institutions in landholding structures and the politics of clientelism and of patronage associated with them, all of which tend to set people in competition against each other rather than encouraging cooperation. But the conclusion which has been drawn from his work is that the Italian South is locked into 'underdevelopment' not because of structural conditions, but because of its relative lack of social capital. Prosperous regions had abundant civic organization whereas poor regions didn't. Without such organizations the poor lacked social capital which in turn undermined political and economic development. Therefore government efforts should be directed at facilitating the development of self-help in the poor regions. The possibility that some redistribution of resources might have a significant part to play both in facilitating local organization and in assisting political and economic development is studiously ignored.

As Putnam's many powerful critics from amongst the ranks of the historians of Italy point out, he also studiously ignores both the evidence that – in the words of a contemporary writer – the Italian South was 'made into the Ireland of Italy' in the political context of the early nineteenth century (i.e., in present-day language was subjected to underdevelopment), and an alternative historiography which explains the performance of regional governments in both north and south in terms of *political* factors. However these and other powerful criticisms of Putnam's work, in terms of method and logic as well as of historical substance, have been systematically ignored, by the author himself and by his followers, and Putnam's book *Making Democracy Work* has become a charter for the view that social capital, understood as meaning essentially 'membership in groups' or 'voluntary associations', is a critical condition for 'good government', and probably for economic development as well.

It is this reasoning which has resonated strongly amongst World Bank specialists who have by now devoted a good deal of energy to demonstrating that 'membership in groups' is 'good for people'. For example, it has been shown that, holding other factors constant, people who are well connected through membership groups are better off than others. One important study found that 'the quantitative effect of social capital [measured in terms of associational activity] is surprisingly large . . . as large as *tripling* either the level of education or stock of non-farming physical assets'.[10] Small wonder, given findings like these, that social capital should have come to be described as the 'missing link' in development; or that so much emphasis should have come to be placed on 'local organization' and 'self-help' – even though this sometimes looks rather like expecting the most disadvantaged people to pull themselves up by their own boot straps, in a way which is remarkably convenient for those who wish to implement large-scale public expenditure cuts.

The idea of the 'missing link' provides strong conceptual support for programmes that emphasize such tasks as 'identifying pockets of social capital (in practice this means 'local' or 'voluntary associations')', and then 'using them and participation to deliver projects'; or for programmes that identify 'the construction of social capital' with 'encouragement for participation'. All this tends to mean 'support for non-governmental organizations (NGOs)' as well, because it quite often turns out that the most prominent and best set-up of local associations are NGOs, though not always ones which are membership organizations. One senior World Bank staffer, off the record, has said that there is preference wherever possible for channelling funds to and through NGOs rather than to local government bodies such as panchayats. The social capital idea helps to justify such a practice. After all, Putnam's study *seems* convincingly to demonstrate that 'social capital' is a condition for the effective functioning of local government. So doesn't it make better sense to build social capital through NGOs rather than by channelling money to local government bodies?

. . . and how does it fit into the 'anti-politics machine'?

Context and power

Much of this seems eminently reasonable and sensible. Of course organization of and by people matters. If by 'social capital' we understand something like 'norms and values of reciprocity and trust', then we can readily see why it is valuable, because it should make cooperation easier. It ought to be worthwhile to have more of it. The kinds of programmes to which I have just referred seem on the face of it impeccably progressive. There are perhaps just a couple of little nagging doubts. One arises from the possibility (the fact, I think) that interpretations of Putnam's Italian work elevate a symptom (relative lack of 'civic engagement' or of 'organization in civil society') into a cause. The second is the concern that the 'local associations' and NGOs, which are brought into so sharp a focus by this interpretation, are not necessarily democratically representative organizations, nor democratically accountable, and might be attractive because they appear to offer the possibility of a kind of democracy through 'popular participation', but without the inconveniences of contestational politics and the conflicts of values and ideas which are a necessary part of democratic politics. The 'anti-politics machine' sits in the wings . . .

And don't we need to look rather carefully at context? There is, after all, a lot of research showing that in circumstances in which – as in the Italian South – assets are unequally distributed, local associations may well be dominated by and used to further the interests of more powerful people. The early history of community development in India – an earlier avatar of 'participation' – demonstrated this very clearly. Latterly, as the practices of Participatory Rural Appraisal have been applied in India, it seems possible that they have had somewhat similar effects. An anthropologist, David Mosse, who has observed PRA exercises very closely in India, shows how in some circumstances they can create arenas in which locally powerful people project their agendas.[11]

In fact the World Bank publication – the one by Christiaan Grootaert, that celebrates the 'missing link' – recognizes these points. There is a reference to the possibility that 'local institutions' may be most effective at enforcing cooperative action 'when the local distribution of assets is more equal'; and that these local institutions 'may be captured by those with local power'. It is recognized, too, that 'The application of social capital in development is not a distribution-neutral process'; and that by themselves – without other resources – these associations may not make very much difference.[12] (Indeed it is perfectly possible to think of groups of people who may have strong social networks and abundant social capital but who are unable to turn it to any advantage because of the context in which they live – people living in inner-city ghettos, for example, or Dalits, those Indians who used to be described as 'untouchables', as opposed to members of dominant castes.) All of which seems very sensible. Yet the paper still concludes with strong recommendations about the role of donors and of governments in promoting 'desirable' forms of social capital, which are in turn equated with 'local-level social capital', local government and NGOs. The caveats are raised but then pushed aside. Three years later, the World Bank's well-presented website on social capital has little or no space for Grootaert's reservations (as I show in chapter 6).

And is there not a 'dark side' to social capital?

There is another set of caveats to the general proclamation of faith in social capital. Clearly the existence of a strong network among a particular group of people – be they Frafra migrants in Accra or, for the sake of argument, Italians in American cities early in the last century – can be a very important resource for them. But does their network necessarily constitute a resource for the society as a whole? When the network is described as a 'mafia', then – it is usually felt – quite clearly not. A moment's reflection shows that 'social capital' for one group of people may constitute 'social exclusion' for others: for example, the 'good jobs' may have become the preserve of a particular ethnic group. Others are deliberately excluded and so are more or less condemned to the poorer jobs – as has happened in the way in which caste or other ethnic affiliations have influenced labour markets.[13] They are in this way subject to 'social exclusion', partly because of the vitality of the social capital, or the strength of the bonds within the other group. This is only one rather specific instance of how particular interests may be organized against the wider social interest. Another American scholar Mancur Olson, writing about ten years before Putnam in a book called *The Rise and Decline of Nations*,[14] argued that well-organized interest groups have indeed no incentive to work towards the common good of society and every incentive to engage in socially costly and inefficient, but privately profitable, 'rent-seeking'. This is a point that seemed to escape Swaminathan S Anklesaria Aiyar when he enthusiastically suggested that caste loyalty constitutes India's most important stock of social capital.

In response to these objections the protagonists of social capital – the faithful, like Swaminathan Aiyar – have said, in effect, 'Yes, we have to recognize that there is a possible "dark side"[15] to social capital.' They then proceed to save the concept by arguing that it is necessary to distinguish between the kind of social capital that binds the members of a group together ('bonding capital') and the sort of social capital, on the other hand, that connects people from different social groups ('bridging capital') – and which works against the exclusive effects which may arise from social capital. Both, they argue, are necessary for development. There is also the possibility of the existence of 'linking capital', or ties between the relatively weak and relatively powerful people 'in positions of influence in formal organizations (banks, agricultural extension offices, the police)'.[16] The last suggestion, in particular, seems an extraordinary expression of the weakness of reasoning that takes no real account of the context of power and of class relations. Ironically, the idea of 'linking capital' is said to have been developed in *response* to the recognition that 'A theory of social capital that focuses only on relations within [bonding] and between [bridging] communities opens itself to the criticism that it ignores power'. Yet the response, while recognizing the exclusion of poorer people 'by overt discrimination or lack of resources from the places where major decisions relating to their welfare are made', is a suggestion which accepts and even celebrates existing differences of wealth and power. There is certainly no dearth of evidence to show how 'linking capital' between particular groups of poorer people and, say, the police (but not only the police) contributes to the reproduction of oppression and of poverty.[17] The protagonists have, it seems, forgotten the lessons in their holy book, *Making Democracy Work*. In describing social relations in the Italian South Putnam emphasizes the importance of patron–client relations, which link some poor people with those in positions of power and influence. These are relations which are seen, rightly, as serving to reinforce existing power relations and therefore as militating against 'civic engagement' and all that is held to follow from it. There could not be a more vivid demonstration of the ways in which the language of social capital is depoliticizing than that which appears in these passages quoted from the World Bank's *World Development Report 2000/2001*. Existing power structures are in fact accepted as given. The possibility that through political organization and mass mobilization – which can both draw upon and help to construct 'social capital' (if you must) – poorer people might actually struggle against 'exclusion' and 'lack of resources', and so bring about change in the distribution of power and resources, does not even enter into consideration.

Finally, it is worth citing a particular case to underline the point. It would not be surprising to find that, following a methodology like Putnam's for Italy, Kerala has the highest levels of 'social capital' among the states of the Indian Union.[18] And the extent of 'public action' in Kerala, involving citizen as well as state action, has been widely celebrated thanks to the work of, among others, Dreze and Sen.[19] Can this public action be understood except by taking into account the history of political mobilization in the state, which was also instrumental in bringing about India's most notable agrarian reform?[20] To use a metaphor which is no doubt rather tired, but still powerfully expressive, it would be like trying to play *Hamlet* without the Prince of Denmark. The idea of social capital has been used, following Robert Putnam's inspiration, to elevate symptom to cause, and to raise, but then push aside, matters that are concerned with the distribution of resources, agrarian production relations and the like. The role of political organization and of political struggle has then been quite systematically downplayed, to the point of being completely air-brushed away.

Conclusion

In this chapter I have outlined the origins and uses of the idea of social capital and the meanings which are ascribed to it – and why it has been described as the 'missing link' in development. It is really rather a simple and familiar notion – that 'connections' ('not what you know but who you know'), norms and values which encourage reciprocity and trust between people are valuable to them, and may sometimes be valuable to the wider society of which they are part (although there is a rather tricky distinction that has to be made between the positive and the negative, the 'upsides' and the 'downsides' – or "dark side" – of these phenomena from the point of view of society as a whole). The invention of the concept of 'social capital' might be thought to be an instance, therefore, of the kind of discovery which has often made for great break-throughs in scholarship, that is, the recognition of the significance of familiar facts. A close examination of the burgeoning literature (which is taken further in this book) shows, however, that elabo-ration of the idea of 'social capital' has mystified rather than clarified. It systematically evades issues of context and power. As I have argued above, therefore, this mystification serves the political purposes of depoliticizing the problems of poverty and social justice and, in elevating the importance of 'voluntary association' in civic engagement, of painting out the need for political action. 'Social capital' is thus a weapon in the armoury of the 'anti-politics machine'.

There is much in these ideas about social capital that is very compelling. Of course the ways in which people relate to each other matter – 'organization' matters – and the resolution of problems of collective action is an absolutely central concern in relation to development as progressive social change as well as to development as economic growth. But this is, after all, what *politics* is about! Action becomes political whenever the help of other people is necessary for an individual to be able to achieve her aim. And it is really not surprising to find that strong associational life can give rise to real and tangible, measurable benefits for people –

even unintended ones. However, the association of these ideas –
and those surrounding 'civil society' and 'participation' – with a
policy (and that means *political*[21]) agenda that continues to cele-
brate the centrality of 'the market' in development, the fantasy of
the 'free' or self-regulating market economy,[22] and the policies of
stabilization and adjustment, gives rise to the kinds of contradictions that are papered over by such weasel words as those I
quoted above concerning 'linking capital', or building ties
between poor people and those in positions of power. The pursuit
of the key economic policies is supported by ideas and activities
which are presented as being about democratic participation, but
which have the effect of depoliticizing and disarming popular
struggles for a more just distribution of resources and opportunities. In the end, as Richard Couto says, in the words of a great
song written in the 1930s by Florence Reece, the wife of a miner
in Harlan County, USA, it comes down to the question of 'Which
Side Are You On?'[23] Those who sincerely want to help the poor
but who are unwilling to contemplate political challenge to existing structures of power (which applies, I suggest, to the authors
of the World Bank Report from which I quoted) end up on the
wrong side.

In the chapters that I follow I will first trace the evolution of the
idea of social capital, concentrating on the work of Robert Putnam
– because it has been so influential – and point up the serious
problems of logic and substantive history in which it is so deeply
mired. I will then follow it through into some other influential
work, mostly coming out of or closely associated with the World
Bank, in the contemporary practices of development. As I do so I
will show the purposes which are served by this discourse, coming
at the end to alternatives which recognize the significance of what
is obscured in these contemporary conceptualizations of 'social
capital'.

2

Where the 'Missing Link' Came From

(or, How a Harvard professor became a celebrity)

*For at least ten centuries, the North and the South have followed con-
trasting approaches to the dilemmas of collective action that afflict all
societies. In the North horizontal civic bonds have undergirded levels of
economic and institutional performance generally much higher than in
the South. This history suggests that both states and markets operate
more efficiently in civic settings.*

Robert Putnam[1]

Robert Putnam's book *Making Democracy Work: civic traditions in modern Italy* (written, in fact, with two others, Robert
Leonardi and Rafaella Nanetti, whose names appear on the title
page in smaller print),[2] was described in a review at the time in
the London *Economist* as being 'a great work of social science'
ranking alongside 'De Tocqueville, Pareto and Max Weber'.
Subsequently, according to no less an authority than the editor of
the distinguished *Quarterly Journal of Economics*, the book became
the most frequently cited work published by a social scientist in
the 1990s.[3] There is no doubt that it was this book that was
responsible for launching the idea of social capital on its meteoric
career even though, ironically, it is clear both from the book and
from academic gossip, that the chapter on 'Social Capital and
Institutional Success' was a late afterthought in a piece of work
which had been long in the making ('social capital' isn't mentioned until this last chapter). *Making Democracy Work* brought
Putnam renown and distinction among social scientists, but his
applications of arguments deriving from his Italian research to his
own country from the mid-1990s onward – work which recently
culminated in the publication of a big book called *Bowling Alone:*

the collapse and revival of American community[4] – actually made him famous. He became a guest of the president and – ultimate of accolades – a TV talk show celebrity.

And yet *Making Democracy Work* was subjected to devastating criticism on grounds of logic, method and substantive historical fact by Putnam's fellow specialists on Italian history and politics and by his peers among American political scientists. None was more devastating, despite its courtesy and generosity, than that of Sidney Tarrow, Professor of Government at Cornell University and author of important books on *Peasant Communism in Italy* and on social movements.[5] Putnam has never responded to these powerful criticisms of his Italian work, except obliquely, and in certain respects his argument about social capital in *Bowling Alone* departs significantly from that in the first book. I was intrigued myself, when first I read *Making Democracy Work*, to find that the argument about social capital is buttressed by reference to the 'amoral familism' in the Italian South, an idea drawn from an old book by Edward C Banfield, called *The Moral Basis of a Backward Society*.[6] This is a book, and an idea, to which I had been introduced in the first course that I ever took at university – but as an object lesson in bad social science.[7] The question of why it is that a book (Putnam's) which has been rather comprehensively rebutted should have been found so powerfully insightful, and thought to be such a masterpiece, calls for an answer. First, however, I will outline Putnam's arguments and will then explain, mainly in the next chapter, the criticisms which have been levelled at *Making Democracy Work*. In a subsequent chapter I shall also review *Bowling Alone* in the same way, because although my concern is primarily with the problem of 'social capital' in the context of 'developing' societies, Putnam's American excursus brings out the implications of the general argument with particular clarity. But let us begin with a short discussion of the antecedents of the idea of 'social capital'.

Social capital before Putnam

The fact that the notion of 'social capital' should have been invented and reinvented on a number of occasions is a tribute, as I suggested earlier, to its inherent, intuitive plausibility and attractiveness. 'The term social capital turns out to have been independently invented at least six times over the twentieth century,' Robert Putnam tells us, 'each time to call attention to the ways in which our lives are made more productive by social ties.' The first use of the idea that has been identified thus far (though surely the notion of our lives 'being made more productive by social ties' is a foundational idea in social and political philosophy?[8]) was in the work, published in 1916, of 'a practical reformer of the Progressive Era [in the United States] – L J Hanifan, state supervisor of rural schools in West Virginia',[9] who urged the importance of community involvement for good schools in a way that has a remarkably contemporary ring to it. Later, according to Caroline Moser, the anthropologist Meyer Fortes, writing in 1958, spoke in terms of social capital;[10] and Jane Jacobs, in her 1961 book *The Death and Life of Great American Cities*,[11] wrote about neighbourliness in these terms. Then in the mid-1970s an economist, Glenn Loury, proposed the idea again in work explaining the determinants of income differences between members of different racial groups in the USA – and his research influenced one of the two principal theoreticians of 'social capital', the American sociologist the late James S Coleman. The other, also a scholar with deep interests in education, though one of an entirely different stamp, is the French anthropologist/sociologist Pierre Bourdieu. It is important to note that Putnam acknowledges Coleman as the principal theorist of social capital, yet makes no reference at all to Bourdieu, who was writing about it well before Coleman. A reading from Coleman is the first of the World Bank's 'Key Readings on Social Capital' (accessible from the Social Capital Website discussed in chapter 6), but the contribution of Bourdieu merits a passing reference in only one of the fifteen papers included in this list.[12] Given that Coleman was an exponent of rational choice theorizing (which in essence applies the reasoning of neo-classical economics to the analysis of other social spheres as well as that of the economy),[13] while Bourdieu is a cultural theorist deeply imbued with Marxist thought and a long-standing concern for the ways in which social class is reproduced, this omission is certainly significant – though perhaps hardly surprising in an institution whose intellectual culture is very largely subject to the hegemony of this brand of economics.[14]

Coleman

James Coleman was a leading exponent of quantitative sociology and the author of a magisterial study called *Foundations of Social Theory*[15] (the latter part of which is specifically devoted to 'The Mathematics of Social Action'). These foundations, for Coleman, lie in a model of individual behaviour, familiar to most of us from elementary neo-classical economics (i.e. the orthodox or conventional economics of virtually all textbooks on the subject), which starts with the axiom that 'Actors have a single principle of action, that of acting so as to maximize their realization of interests'.[16] Coleman, therefore, is a methodological individualist – one, it must be said, of subtlety and distinction. And the model of individual behaviour to which he refers is the elementary model of rational choice theory which is now extremely influential in political science and sociology, especially in the United States. The axiom itself immediately exposes one of the problems with this (evidently powerful) approach in the social sciences: how are 'interests' defined? Surely they cannot be defined outside a social and cultural context that is itself historically given? The frame of thought tends to tautology: interests are what people appear to be trying to maximize.

Coleman's formulation of the idea of social capital of course reflects his theoretical stance.[17] He starts with Loury's work in which, he explains, 'social capital is [taken to mean] the set of resources that inhere in family relations and in community social organization and that are useful for the cognitive or social development of a child or young person',[18] and this is how he himself used the concept in explaining variations in performance in the school system.[19] He goes on to specify that social capital refers to aspects of social structure that constitute 'a capital asset for the individual':

> Social capital is defined by its function. It is not a single entity, but a variety of different entities having two characteristics in common: they all consist of some aspect of social structure, and they facilitate certain actions of the individuals who are within the structure. Like other forms of capital, social capital is productive, making possible the attainment of certain ends that would not be attainable in its absence.

Like physical and human capital, social capital is not completely fungible, but is fungible with respect to specific activities. A given form of social capital that is valuable in facilitating certain actions may be useless or even harmful for others [this is the 'downside' or 'dark side' that we encountered in the previous chapter]. Unlike other forms of capital, social capital inheres in the structure of relations between persons and among persons. It is lodged neither in individuals nor in physical implements of production.[20]

A number of examples are then offered to illustrate different forms of social capital: the way in which student activism in South Korea was built on study circles formed by groups of students coming from the same home town or high school or church; the apparent decline in trust in the relationships between doctors and patients in the United States; the greater sense of security felt by a mother of young children in Jerusalem as compared with Detroit, because 'In Jerusalem the normative structure ensures that unattended children will be looked after by adults in the vicinity';[21] and the relationships obtaining between merchants in the central market in Cairo where, we are told, 'family relations are important'.[22] This last example may recall, for those familiar with sociological studies of Indian business, David Rudner's work on Nattukottai Chettiars (or Nakarattars). The conclusion of Rudner's book actually has the title 'Social Structure as Social Investment', which sums up his argument that '. . . the Nakarattar banking system was a caste-based banking system. Individual Nakarattars organized their lives around participation in and management of various communal institutions adapted to the task of accumulating and distributing reserves of [money] capital'.[23]

Coleman's examples – and Rudner's ethnography, one chapter title of which evokes the idea – suggest that 'social capital' refers to trust, or the norms of reciprocity which the idea of trust entails. This seems to be confirmed in what he goes on to argue about how and why social relations can constitute useful 'capital' for individuals. He highlights: (i) the significance of insurance, related to the obligations and expectations which arise in social relationships (so that rational individuals create obligations among others, that come to function like 'credit slips'); (ii) the information that is communicated through social relations;[24] and (iii) the ways in which the existence of norms and effective sanctions facilitates action, by reducing transaction costs in various ways. Here, one very clearly sees continuities between Coleman's reasoning and that of the type of microeconomics currently very influential in the World Bank. This is also founded on propositions about information.[25]

When social relationships concentrate effective power then social capital may be created for all the members of the group concerned because of the overcoming of free-rider problems (as seems to be the case among the Nakarattas, people generally don't dare to 'free-ride' on others by failing to reciprocate). But beyond this specific case, Coleman argues, much social capital is a public good. This means that it is not necessarily in any individual's interest to bring it into being, and in fact 'most forms of social capital are created or destroyed as a by-product of other activities'.[26] But there are also some forms of social capital which are the result of deliberate investment by people, such as in business organizations or voluntary associations like parent–teacher organizations, where those concerned 'have the aim of receiving a return on their investment',[27] whether or not there are also externalities which benefit non-participants (as may well be the case with Parent Teacher Associations, for example. The existence of a strong PTA may benefit parents who are not members, and their children). Coleman's conceptualization of social capital, therefore, suggests the possibility of 'building' social capital by encouraging investment in organizations of this kind. But it also makes it apparent – uncomfortably, for his own broader theoretical position – that the implications of social capital differ according to circumstances and for different groups of people. It is certainly not clear that these are resources which can be accumulated, transferred or inherited in the way which is true of other forms of capital (as they are defined by Coleman).

Bourdieu

Bourdieu's idea of 'social capital' is more subtle, though it may not appear so at first glance.[28] He writes:

> One can give an intuitive idea of it by saying that it is what ordinary language calls 'connections' . . . by constructing this concept one acquires the means of analysing the logic

whereby this particular kind of capital is accumulated, transmitted and reproduced, the means of understanding how it turns into economic capital and, conversely, what work is required to convert economic capital into social capital, the means of grasping the function of institutions such as clubs or, quite simply, the family, the main site of accumulation and transmission of that kind of capital.[29]

Bourdieu has a rather chaotic conception of 'capital' which leans in some ways towards the conventional view of it as 'stuff used to produce things', or as 'assets', but also holds that it comes in many forms. He is in fact especially concerned with 'cultural capital' – referring to socially constructed qualifications of one sort or another, to which rank is attached – and with 'symbolic capital', which refers to prestige or honour. Social capital, for Bourdieu, is intimately linked to these forms of capital, which enter significantly into the formation and reproduction of class. As I put it earlier, the 'possession' of durable social relationships is both a condition of differential access to resources and an aspect of social differentiation. Cultural/symbolic/social capital are, quite evidently, 'socially and historically limited to the circumstances that create them . . . they are contextual and constructed'. Thus, while Bourdieu's concept of social capital as 'connections' seems to put him in sympathy with 'the new economic sociology', and with the work of Mark Granovetter in particular – which we shall encounter again very shortly, as a significant influence on Putnam, and whose focus (like Coleman's) is on social networks – for Bourdieu it is not enough to establish the existence of a network; it is also essential to examine its cultural/ideological content and context. As I shall explain, a very important aspect of Putnam's reworking of the idea of social capital is that content and context are stripped out. The Bourdieuvian concept is not one that recommends itself to the World Bank specialists whose views and arguments were introduced in the previous chapter. The concept that has proven attractive to them is not of phenomena that are ideologically or contextually – and therefore historically – dependent. 'Social capital can only reign supreme by excising the cultural, the symbolic – and Bourdieu.'[30]

As I have put it, if Bourdieu and Coleman have been the philosophers of social capital, one from the camp of the rational choice theorists, the other from that of historically grounded cultural theory, Robert Putnam has been its High Priest, simplifying and popularizing, and ministering unto a diverse and rapidly expanding flock of followers. We should turn to him.

Putnam's Italian circularities

Putnam and his collaborators studied the performance of regional governments in Italy from their establishment in 1970 (so that *Making Democracy Work* is the fruit of more than twenty years of research, which involved a variety of large-scale surveys and a number of different sorts of case studies). Their work, which actually merits detailed methodological study, includes both quite elaborate statistical analyses and a review of Italian historiography. Essentially, they claim to have demonstrated that the most important single determinant of the performance of these democratic regional governments, *and* of differing levels of socio-economic development in the different regions of Italy, is the factor that they label variously as 'civic involvement', 'civic engagement' or 'civic tradition', as given by a measure of 'civic community'. Indeed 'civic involvement 1900s' (i.e. around 1900) predicts 'socio-economic development 1970s' more strongly than does 'socio-economic development 1900s'. 'A region's chances of achieving socio-economic development during this century [as of having effective democratic government] have depended less on its initial socio-economic endowments than on its civic endowments [level of 'civic involvement']. In so far as we can judge . . . the contemporary correlation between civics and economics [i.e. between 'civic involvement' and levels of socio-economic development] reflects primarily the impact of civics on economics, not the reverse.'[31]

The argument proceeds as follows:

1. Measures are derived from the performance of different regional governments in terms of: *government processes* (cabinet stability; the promptness with which budgets have been passed; the quality of statistical and information services); the *content of policy decisions* (reform legislation); and of *policy implementation* (service delivery given by numbers of day care centres in operation by December 1983, standardized by the population of

children aged zero to four, and the number of family clinics in operation, comparably standardized; industrial policy instruments in place; and three measures of the effectiveness of regional governments at using funds offered to them by the central government). There is a fairly high degree of inter-correlation between these indices and a composite measure is derived, which is also shown to correspond well with the results of opinion surveys on the levels of satisfaction with government of both ordinary citizens and community leaders. 'Institutional performance' in this sense (meaning 'government performance') is clearly highest in north-central Italy and lowest in the South.

2. It is then shown that 'institutional [government] performance' is highly correlated with a measure of 'civic engagement', the 'civic community index' that is composed by (what are shown to be) the highly inter-correlated variables of:

- preference voting 1953–79
- referendum turnout 1974–87
- newspaper readership 1975
- scarcity [/density] of sports and cultural associations 1981

Influenced by de Tocqueville's view, expressed in his *Democracy in America* (the book based on his visits in the 1830s) of the great importance of Americans' 'propensity' to form organizations of diverse kinds, because they 'contribute to the effectiveness and stability of democratic government . . . both [through] their "internal" effects on members and because of their "external" effects on the wider polity',[32] Putnam and his fellow authors were especially interested in the density of voluntary associations. The effects of such associations, they say, 'do not require that the manifest purpose of the association be political. Taking part in a choral society or a bird-watching club can teach self-discipline and an appreciation for the joys of successful collaboration'.[33] And they found that in some regions of Italy people seem to be as much congenital 'joiners' as are Americans, whereas elsewhere – especially the South – they are not. The significance of newspaper readership, also remarked upon by de Tocqueville, is fairly self-evident in regard to 'civic engagement'; the reasons for the incorporation of the other two indices are perhaps less clear. Electoral turnout is not a good measure of political participation in Italy, as it is elsewhere – the United States, for example – because until relatively recently Italian law required citizens to vote in general elections, whereas there has been no such condition in regard to the referenda that have been regularly conducted since 1974. Therefore the measure of turnout in referenda is used. Finally, preference voting is included (as an inverse correlate of civic engagement) because 'it has long been acknowledged by students of Italian politics as a reliable indicator of personalism, factionalism and patron–client politics'[34] – which are the antithesis of 'civic engagement'. 'Civic community', thus measured, is shown to be highly correlated with government performance; and:

3. Statistical analysis demonstrates the conclusion that I reported earlier, concerning the explanation of both government performance and socio-economic development by this factor.

Quite contrary to the expectations of the classical social theorists who saw modernity as 'the enemy of civility' (or of a sense of 'community'), 'the least civic areas of Italy are precisely the traditional southern villages'.[35] Putnam traces the roots of the very marked differences that he finds, through the period after Unification in the late nineteenth and early twentieth centuries (for which measures of civic involvement show an 'almost perfect correlation' with the civic community index for the 1970s and 1980s), right back to the Middle Ages and the establishment of the Norman feudal kingdom in the south, while communal republicanism grew up, meanwhile, in the cities of northern and central Italy (like Florence, Genoa, Pisa and Siena).

'Virtuous' North, 'Vicious' South

Putnam argues, then, that the South has been locked into a vicious spiral in which social institutions, such as those of clientelism and patron–client relations, in the context of a feudal agararian structure both gave rise to and represent a response to pervasive mistrust. Peasants were in competition with each other for the best strips of land and 'Vertical relationships between patron and client, and obsequiousness to the landlord, were more important than horizontal solidarities'.[36] As Geof Wood has argued, these sorts of social relationships in a sense represent a kind of 'adverse incorporation' in social networks.[37] Putnam's account draws support from Banfield's notion of 'amoral familism', developed in

The Moral Basis of a Backward Society, a book that was based on field research in a rural town in the far south that he called Montegrano. 'Extreme poverty and backwardness [in Montegrano],' Banfield suggested, 'is to be explained largely by the inability of villagers to act together for the common good or, indeed, for any end transcending the immediate material interest of the nuclear family. This inability to concert activity beyond the immediate family arises from an ethos – that of "amoral familism" [meaning 'maximize the material short-term advantage of the nuclear family and assume that all others will do likewise'], produced by three factors acting in combination: a high death rate, certain land tenure conditions and the absence of the institution of the extended family.'[38] The problems with this idea have to do with the way in which it allocates causal primacy to an 'ethos' rather than to the material conditions that gave rise to it.

Of the South Putnam writes, 'Force [private violence was deployed by the southern feudal nobility to reinforce dominance and dependency] and family provide a primitive substitute for civic community. This equilibrium has been the tragic fate of southern Italy for a millennium.'[39] The north and centre, on the other hand, have experienced a long history in which the existence of 'networks of civic engagement' and of 'norms of generalised reciprocity' have given rise to a virtuous spiral of 'brave reciprocity' (as opposed to the maxim of 'always defect' which is implicit in southern 'amoral familism'):

> Social trust, norms of reciprocity, networks of civic engagement, and successful cooperation are mutually reinforcing. [Note that the lumping-together of these under the label of 'social capital' was an afterthought.] Effective collaborative institutions require interpersonal skills and trust, but those skills and trust are also inculcated and reinforced by organized collaboration.[40]

There is, therefore, 'path dependence' (in the sense in which Douglass North and others have used this term[41]) and 'Where norms and networks of civic engagement are lacking the outlook for civic engagement looks bleak. The fate of the Mezzogiorno is an object lesson for the Third World today and the former communist lands of Eurasia tomorrow'.[42] The problem with

which Putnam leaves his readers is that of the constructability of
what he calls, only at the last, 'social capital', in circumstances –
like those of the Italian South – where it has been missing historically. He argues that the changes that have taken place in the
formal political institutions of Italy have had a positive effect,
even though 'The new institution [of regional government] has
not yet lived up to the highest expectations of its optimistic advocates'. And the final lesson from this research is, he says, 'that
most institutional history moves slowly'.[43] For those concerned
with social and economic development, therefore, the findings of
the Putnam study are ambiguous: on the one hand it demonstrates the importance of social organization (social capital as the
'missing link' in development), but on the other hand it suggests
that those societies that have been burdened historically with
ineffective and inefficient institutions may not easily shift onto
another path on which the virtuous spiral of 'brave reciprocity'
will flourish. This ambiguity is an extension of the uneasy and
in the end unsatisfactory way in which Putnam's use of the notion
of 'path dependence' aims to resolve the problems of action
and structure: it seems that actors do make choices at some
point but that they are subjected thereafter to a deterministic,
even culturalist, logic.

Where does 'social capital' come from?

There is a confessed circularity about the argument ('the culture-
vs.-structure, chicken-and-egg debate is ultimately fruitless'[44]):
'norms of generalized reciprocity' and 'networks of civic engagement' give rise to social capital, which in turn makes cooperation
between people possible, and reinforces reciprocity and civic
engagement. How the problems of collective action that constrain
reciprocity and civic engagement are overcome in the first place is
a problem that is not addressed, and indeed it is stated that 'where
no prior example of successful civic collaboration exists, it is more
difficult to overcome barriers of suspicion and shirking'.[45]

The only way out of this circularity is in the strong suggestion
that civic engagement arises from 'weak' horizontal ties, such as
loose ties of acquaintance rather than the 'strong' ties of family,
kinship or neighbourhood. Putnam follows Granovetter[46] in
arguing that:

'strong' interpersonal ties (like kinship and intimate friendship) are less important than 'weak' ties (like acquaintanceship and shared membership in secondary associations) in sustaining collective action. Dense but segregated horizontal networks sustain cooperation within each group, but networks that cut across social cleavages [such as are created in sports clubs, mutual aid societies, cultural associations and voluntary unions] nourish wider cooperation.[47]

This is the closest that Putnam gets to theorizing social capital. Note that it is distinctly odd, in the light of this emphatic statement, that he should refer elsewhere, and so approvingly – as in his American work – to the importance of strong interpersonal ties like those in Chinese family networks, which would not seem to 'nourish wider cooperation'.[48] But it is reflection on these ideas that has given rise to the distinction which has been made latterly, as I explained in the previous chapter, between 'bonding' and 'bridging' capital – a distinction which is perhaps anticipated in the passage I have quoted. Here, however, it is clearly argued that it is because membership in 'horizontal' voluntary associations cuts across 'social cleavages' that the associations are so vital in 'making democracy work'. The sorts of social networks created by these associations build reciprocity; this in turn is the foundation for trust which is, Putnam says, 'an essential component of social capital'.[49] There is no suggestion that the content (or explicit purpose or ideology) of 'association' makes any difference, or that there are any aspects of the context of different associations which matter.

These ideas about social capital, seen as arising out of interpersonal relationships but also as extending, in some way which is never specified, to the wider society (the centre-north of Italy is held to have more of it than 'the south'), are developed in the final chapter (chapter 6) of *Making Democracy Work*. In earlier chapters, when he discusses the formation of 'civicness' or 'civic engagement', Putnam at least mentions the role of public institutions. Civic republicanism, it seems, depended not only on the existence of vigorous associational networks but also on people's confidence 'that contracts and the laws governing them would be impartially enforced'. Laws, and courts – institutions of government – to administer them, and people's *confidence* in these institutions, also played a part in forming civic virtue. In chapter 6, however, the argument we are offered is narrowly society-centred. The possible contributions of public institutions, and therefore of government, to the formation of social capital are more or less forgotten and, it seems, the lines of causality run only in one direction – from society, specifically horizontal voluntary association, to government performance, and presumably the functioning of democracy. In some of his later writings Putnam explicitly seeks to distance himself from this interpretation, saying for example that 'progressives [as he labels himself] should resist the view that government can be replaced by civil society'.[50] But the damage is done in the final chapter of *Making Democracy Work*, and his society-centric argument came to lend power to the elbows of conservative 'rollers-back of the state' both in the United States and in the international development establishment.

Conclusion

In this chapter I have given an account of the development of the concept of 'social capital'. Though I have shown that there are differences in the ways in which the term has been used by its three most influential expositors, Bourdieu, Coleman and then Putnam the popularizer, it clearly refers to resources that inhere in social relationships. They are resources otherwise labelled as 'trust' and 'reciprocity', that both underlie and derive from some social networks. In an extended account of Robert Putnam's much-lauded book on Italian politics, *Making Democracy Work*, I have shown how this in essence rather simple idea has been developed, and associated in particular with 'horizontal, voluntary association' in civil society (flippantly, with choirs, football clubs and bird-watching societies); and then deployed as an explanation for both economic and governmental performance in different regions of Italy.

The broad conclusions that have been drawn from Putnam's 'Italian job', and which help to account for its extraordinary success, are (i) that it shows that organization in civil society crucially influences (determines?) the functioning both of government (and democracy), and of the economy; and (ii) that it suggests that unequal conditions flow *from* variations in social capital. As I argued in chapter 1, it seems to show that 'Without civic organizations, the poor lacked social capital, which in turn undermined political and economic activity. Government policies [therefore] are better directed at encouraging local self-help efforts than at redistributing social and economic resources more equally'.[51] This is certainly the inspiration drawn from *Making Democracy Work* by the World Bank specialists on social capital. The next chapter shows just how mistaken these conclusions are.

3

The Fragility of the Foundations

(or, Why the Harvard professor's idea is so misleading)

Social scientists ignore history at their peril; but when we go to history, we must be aware that our models affect what we look for, how we interpret it, and how we conjoin it to our own data . . . (in this case) the historical evidence can be read [just as well] as support for the idea that the nineteenth-century popular politics of north-central Italy are themselves the source of both the civic community and the positive political performance of its regional governments.

Sidney Tarrow[1]

Making Democracy Work won prizes galore and gave currency to the idea of social capital. Critical scrutiny of the book shows up, however, the deep flaws in this idea and its uses. 'Social capital' is in a fact a very doubtful label for quite familiar notions. The phenomena that are thus labelled mean nothing ('social capital' is devoid of meaningful content), except in relation to social and political contexts that have to be historically specified. In the book itself there are problems of method (in the construction of measures, selection of data, and the like); problems of logic (notably in the apparent equation of interpersonal trust generated in face-to-face relationships with generalized trust); and questions of historical substance. I shall start with the latter because Putnam's historiography exposes his ideological project. What is really quite extraordinary is that an argument that has been so comprehensively trashed (this is not too strong a word for it) – even though ever so politely – by the author's fellow specialists should have gone on to enjoy such widespread influence.

A significant (mis)reading of Italian history

'Historical path dependence' as a substitute for historical analysis

Robert Putnam has expressed irritation in his response to some of the criticisms of *Making Democracy Work* that have come from historians of Italy. After all, the part of the book which traces back to the Middle Ages the roots of the differences of civic engagement that he discerns between the Italian North and South is short, and not really essential to his main arguments. And there are – of course – many differences of opinion amongst Italian historians themselves. This may be so, but Putnam's reading of history shows up the ideological underpinnings of his arguments rather starkly. It also highlights the classic failing of social scientists when they turn to history, namely, their strong tendency to substitute a model or a stereotyped set of sociological generalizations for historical analysis.[2] In Putnam's case, he projects a stereotyped idea of social and political differences between 'the North' and 'the South' of Italy, each of them treated as if it were an homogeneous entity, which holds that the former has a 'virtuous' dynamic and the latter a 'vicious' one – an idea which is itself ideologically rooted in Italian history[3] – across a millennium. The contrasts between the two regions are reinforced in the rhetoric with which he describes them. As that most courteous but still most damning of his critics, Sidney Tarrow, says, some of the descriptions of the Centre-North 'verge on chamber-of-commerce enthusiasm', while 'Putnam's prose in describing the South is as bleak as his language about the Centre-North was elegaic'.[4] It is rather unfortunate for Putnam, then, that some recent events in Italy, notably the corruption scandals involving politicians and business people from the Centre-North rather than the South, belie his characterizations. It is, after all, the 'South' that is supposed to be characterized by corruption. It is also unfortunate for the argument that more recent evidence than that to which Putnam refers should have shown vigorous growth of voluntary associations in the south since 1980.

Yet Putnam proposes ('argues' would be too flattering a verb), rather casually, that the two regions of Italy are locked into 'historical path dependence'. This is a fashionable idea which derives from the work of some economic historians who have shown how past events may constrain present choices ('men making history though not in circumstances of their own choosing' was how an earlier writer put it) and who thus explain how it may be that inefficient technologies or inefficient institutions persist despite the existence of superior alternatives. One classic essay is that of Paul David who explains in a paper on 'the economics of QWERTY' how and why it is that English-language typewriters have long had such a curious arrangement of letters – even though it is not a pattern that is conducive to efficiency.[5] The idea of 'path dependence' in studies such as David's is used with analytical rigour. But Putnam uses it more as a metaphor, with the result that, in spite of his own claims to the contrary, the argument smacks strongly of cultural determinism. The 'North' and the 'South' are each imbued with a distinct cultural essence that can be traced back over a thousand years.[6] This has the objectionable consequence, as I remarked in chapter 1, of implying that Italians were active social agents at some point in the past, 'making their own history', but that they have subsequently become locked for centuries 'in predetermined games of life', like culturally programmed automatons. It also reflects an implicit understanding of 'culture' – as a kind of an unchanging 'essence' – that has been subjected to withering critique by anthropologists and others. 'Culture' should rather been seen as referring to bodies of ideas, symbols and values which are always subject to contestation within the field of social power in any society, and which are therefore never 'complete' but always changing historically.[7]

Putnam, however, absolves himself of 'the responsibility of looking at how and which history matters over time'.[8] He never stops to consider, for example, how and why it turned out that the Norman kingdom of Sicily should not have enjoyed the same subsequent development as that other well-known Norman kingdom – of England.[9] There is in fact a great deal of historical evidence to confound Putnam's stereotypes of the differences between North and South, and to show that the differences which undeniably do exist may well be the product of relatively recent historical events in which the state and political processes have had a central role. Of course we have to do here with interpretations of history, and my point is not to assert that another interpretation than that which Putnam proposes is 'right'. My purpose is to show – following Tarrow, whom I have cited at the head of this chapter, and others – that an interpretation reversing Putnam's lines of causality, and suggesting that state institutions and political processes account *both* for differences in 'civicness' and for what is presumed by Putnam to follow from these differences, is at least as convincing. This, I think, shows up the ideological character of Putnam's project. His case is certainly 'not proven', and I would submit before any jury that his critics have shown that it is an unlikely – indeed, a fantastic – fabrication.

Errors of omission and commission

A special issue of the *Journal of Interdisciplinary History* in 1999 was devoted to Putnam's work. The editor, Robert Rotberg, credits him with having 'modernized [whatever that means in this context] and refined social capital as an analytical tool', implying that it is an instrument of great value for historical analysis.[10] But in fact most of the contributions by historians are not at all 'hospitable' to Putnam's propositions. Two historians of the Renaissance and early modern Italy, writing in the collection, find Putnam's representations of what the north Italian city-states were like before the nineteenth-century Risorgimento quite fanciful. Far from exhibiting cooperation and mutual trust, Brucker argues, 'Republican communes were rife with factionalism, brutality, and authoritarianism. The oligarchies that ran them demanded strong, intrusive government that could curb violence. They trusted regulation, not each other . . . [and] the Medici grand dukes [of Florence] eradicated civil society, as did others in other communes. Absolutism, not republicanism, was the rule'.[11] Tarrow makes much the same point, arguing that 'after a short period as voluntary associations' most of the Italian city-states 'produced closed urban oligarchies'. Putnam's history, he says, 'is telescopic, to say the least'. And why – by what rules of evidence – did Putnam look for the origins of the apparent civic superiority of centre-north Italy 800 years ago rather than in other periods ('its 1919–21 generation of fascism', among others)?[12]

If Putnam uses a kind of historical telescope it also apparent that he sometimes puts it up to a blind eye. This is one of the

main points made in Sabetti's lengthy review. Putnam's stereotypes of virtuous 'North' and vicious 'South' are overdrawn and
get things wrong. If other historians have been concerned about
the romanticism in Putnam's portrayals of the north Italian city-
states, Sabetti supplies a weight of evidence showing that the
South was not always lacking in either associations or civicness.
Putnam neglects the evidence of communal self-government in
the South, for example in graziers' associations in the Middle
Ages, when 'what emerges from the historical record of the par-
liament of graziers is the rich associational life that allowed the
graziers to put aside or resolve their differences and to confront
their common enemies together'. He does not recognize that
church-affiliated organizations in the South, in the words of a
British historian writing in 1904, 'represented, in a curious form,
the embryo of democratic institutions'. He does not acknowledge discordant observations such as the fact that by 1922 'the
three regions comprising what is now Calabria [south] had as
many rural credit institutions started and operated locally as did
Tuscany [centre-north]'. Or acknowledge, and reflect upon the
significance of the fact that 'in the Capitanata region of Apulia
[south] there emerged a labour movement stronger and more
powerful than its counterpart in Emilia Romagna [north, and
top dog for civic community according to Putnam]'. A movement
of landless workers that started in Apulia in the late nineteenth
century had by the early part of the last century created a powerful union, which maintained a high level of internal democracy as
it spread. 'In contrast, by 1920 the workers' leagues in the Po
valley [centre-north] had become so centralized and hierarchical
in nature as to be quite unresponsive to local members', and they
were quickly broken before the advance of fascism. Those of
Apulia, by contrast, contested the fascists 'town by town' in the
1920s. Sabetti suggests that 'it seems evident that the Apulian
land workers had built more solid foundations for generalized
norms of reciprocity and networks of association than had their
counterparts in Emilia Romagna'.[13]

What causes what?

But most significantly, Putnam does not confront the evidence
showing, says Sabetti, that 'The phenomenon of southern

latifundism [the agrarian structure I referred to in my review of Putnam's arguments in chapter 2], far from being a relic of medieval times, is of more recent origin in the intended and unintended consequences of the political changes in the nineteenth century'. It was these changes that created the socio-political conditions in the South to which Putnam refers, and that were described by a contemporary as the 'iron circle' of economic and civil oppression.[14] Tarrow extends the point, referring to the fact that until Unification the Italian South knew nothing but 'foreign' rule and government that reflected 'a logic of colonial exploitation' – which did not suddenly disappear in 1861. He asks:

> How could Robert Putnam, who knows the history of Italian Unification well, have missed the penetration of southern Italian society by the northern state and the effect this had on the region's level of civic competence? The reason seems to lie in *the model with which he turned to history, a model that conceived of civic capacity as a native soil in which state structures grow rather than one being shaped by patterns of state building and state strategy* [my emphasis].[15]

Tarrow's point here recalls exactly one put by Theda Skocpol with reference to Putnam's American studies (see chapter 4). She provides detailed evidence showing that the growth of voluntary associations in the United States, too, was shaped by the pattern of state-building, rather than reflecting – as popular wisdom has had it – the weakness of the national state.

What, Tarrow also asks, do the measures of civic community that Putnam constructs for the later nineteenth century signify? Is it a matter of chance that they are 'strongest in the areas of the Po Valley in which popular politics, both socialist and Catholic, took hold in the late nineteenth century'? The answer he says, is most emphatically 'no' – it was not a matter of chance – for both the Catholic and the socialist parties had deliberate strategies of creating 'just the kind of secondary associations that make up Putnam's measures of civic capacity'. And the impressive correlations that Putnam interprets as showing a causal link across time (and as demonstrating path dependence in operation) can just as well be interpreted as showing that there was a strong correlation between progressive politics and civic performance in the nineteenth century, and that there is also a similar strong connection in the present. As a matter of fact, 'Civic competence was deliberately developed after World War II [in the centre-north; just as it was by the progressive parties in the same region in the later nineteenth century] as a symbol of the left wing parties' governing capacity.' On the other hand, 'Both progressive politics and civic capacity were correspondingly weak in the South.'[16]

A further, most interesting perspective on Putnam's historical analysis has been developed in recent work by Peter Mayer, who has shown that 'almost ninety per cent of economic difference apparent in Italy in the late 1930s could be predicted from female literacy rates of the 1870s',[17] while these female literacy rates were also strongly associated with levels of civic community that emerged in the later nineteenth and early twentieth centuries. And three-quarters of the variation in 'civic community' in Italy today, according to Putnam's measure of this, is explained by female literacy in 1871, and almost two-thirds of the variation in the performance of Italian regional governments. In comparing Indian states, Mayer went on to construct for his research on India comparable measures to those worked by Putnam for Italy. Here again he found that levels of female literacy (in 1951) explain a lot of both 'civic community' and of government performance at later dates. He concludes, 'In the Indian context, levels of education are more important [than social capital]' – which carries the implication that (in the Italian case, as well as in the Indian) the nature of civil society is itself conditioned by state policies and hence by politics.

The following conclusions from the historians' reviews of evidence are strongly supported:

*Putnam's historical model, of virtuous North and vicious South, as long-running historically path-dependent social systems, rests on shaky foundations, conceptually and empirically.

*There is a lot of evidence suggesting that the differences that Putnam identifies between north and south, in terms of 'civic community', are the result of relatively recent historical events having to do with processes of state-building.

*This evidence in turn suggests that, rather than 'civicness' providing the 'soil' (or the foundations, in other words) in which different state structures grow, causality runs in the opposite direction.

This last point is further reinforced by consideration of the question of how, exactly, a 'culture (or a history) of association' influences democracy. The title of Putnam's book promises that it is about democracy. But in fact he and his collaborators measure and try to explain the policy performance of regional governments in Italy, which is not at all the same thing as democratic practice. In the end, as Tarrow concludes, their book actually has 'little to say about democracy'. This is because they are never concerned with the purpose or the content of association and, as James Putzel has said, 'The networks and relationships bred by association do not in themselves guarantee political outcomes.' There surely is a difference between associations like sports clubs and those which have social and political purposes? As Putzel notes – and as I have mentioned above – the supposed associational legacy of northern Italy 'did little to thwart the rise of fascism'.[18] In another context, is there any reason to believe that the social networks and strong associations among the overseas Chinese in various South East Asian countries have been at all conducive to their democratization? The question of what associations are *for* has to be addressed.

Putnam's evident reluctance to accept that the content of association matters – or in other words that *politics* matters – is reflected in his response to the fact that measures of civic community in Italy are also closely correlated with the size of the Communist vote. He and his collaborators concede that 'certainly in a descriptive sense, our evidence is consistent with the judgement, widely held across party lines in Italy, that Communist regions are better governed than most others'. They sought to show that 'Communist regional governments were more successful because they tilled more fertile soil [regions with a strong associational legacy]', but they then found that 'the correlation between PCI power and institutional performance was not entirely attributable to covariance with the civic community'. It remains an awkward possibility (for him), therefore, that the strength of the Communist party is a factor in explaining variations *both* in government performance and in 'civic engagement' – which, remember – Tarrow tells us – was deliberately encouraged by left parties after the Second World War.[19]

There are, therefore, serious problems of historical evidence and interpretation in Putnam's analysis. It is hard not to agree with Tarrow's suggestion that it is all driven by a model which accords causal primacy to 'civic engagement' – in a way that is both historically, and (as I shall show) logically, indefensible. Further, serious doubt is cast upon the argument by Goldberg's demonstration that the factor of civic community, as it is defined by Putnam's index, does not explain variations *within* the 'North' and the 'South', which it clearly should do if it has the explanatory power that Putnam suggests.[20] Let me turn, then, to the problems of logic in Putnam's use of the idea of social capital.

(Mis)Conceptualizing trust and social capital

Although *Making Democracy Work* ends up by suggesting that the Italian 'North' and 'South' have distinct political cultures, it does advance a structural argument, as I explained towards the end of the last chapter. Membership in horizontal voluntary associations builds social networks that cut across social cleavages. Social networks build up reciprocity, and norms of reciprocity make for trust, which Putnam says 'is an essential component of social capital'. He does not define what he means by 'trust', and it is a matter on which a good deal of scholarly ink has been spilled in recent years (partly as a result of this unsatisfactory aspect of his work). Generally, however, it is considered that trust comes into play in situations of uncertainty, when someone takes a step in relation to another, not knowing for sure how that other will respond, but in the belief that the other will act in conformity with her expectations (and so will not take advantage of the vulnerability which is occasioned by her ignorance/uncertainty as to the other's motives). If there is a lot of trust/social capital in a society then it seems that people are more likely to cooperate with each other and to get into the kind of virtuous spiral that Putnam describes as being characteristic of the Italian 'North', associated with better government performance (though through what specific mechanisms is not entirely clear, it must be said).

In somewhat more detail: as a result of the many 'weak ties' between them that are created through their membership in sports associations, choirs and clubs of different kinds, people build up knowledge about each other, and come to rely upon each other. To give a simple illustration: I am probably less likely to let someone else down or to cheat her if we regularly play together in the same football team, are members of the same church choir and also go to the same coffee shop after work. For one thing, through these different connections I form an assessment of her character and I have a shrewd idea of how far I can rely on her in different situations. For another she is likely to reciprocate if I do her a favour of some kind (and vice versa) because of our ongoing connections. In these circumstances there are 'sanctions against my defection' (from an obligation to reciprocate), perhaps because I wouldn't want it to be known around the football club that I can't be relied upon; and there are incentives for me to reciprocate because I can be fairly confident that I'll be able to go on getting help from the other person at different times in the future. These sorts of face-to-face relationships, in other words, are conducive to the development of interpersonal trust.

But how does the trust which may be built up through such kinds of personal relationships become extended to the wider society – which is what Putnam says has happened in the 'North'? I know that I can trust Kate because of all the information that I have about her, and my experience of playing games with her, singing with her and so on. But why should that make me trust someone whom I don't know? There is indeed a good deal of evidence from economic history and from anthropology suggesting that it is perfectly possible for there to be high levels of trust *within* a particular social group – among the Nattukottai Chettiars of south India, perhaps – without this extending beyond the boundaries of the group. To the contrary, it may be that, outside the group, mistrust prevails. This is what the sociologist Satish Saberwal has argued – controversially – is generally characteristic of Indian society, and he sees it as being among the 'roots of crisis' in contemporary India.[21] Putnam has no answer to the question of how interpersonal trust can become generalized trust, beyond the implicit suggestions both that people acquire habits of mind – that those in societies with lots of voluntary association are more inclined to be trusting of others in

general – and that there are positive externalities from cooperation in associations. But how and why membership in one
association necessarily 'leads to overcoming free rider problems
in another is problematic'.[22] And it is clear that there is no simple
process of aggregation whereby the interpersonal trust between
the members of lots of football clubs (say) adds up to generalized
societal trust. Far from it, when it is evident that the reciprocity
and trust within one group may be built up through the exclusion
of others.

Putnam's implicit suggestions may be fair enough in themselves, but they are very weak. Are there not other conditions –
even if they don't have to do with voluntary associations – which
give rise to more generalized trust in a society? For example, it is
possible that a shared identity provides a basis for trusting a
stranger, or shared beliefs. Trust may be based upon common
religious allegiance, or upon a shared political ideology. But isn't
it also possible, exactly as Putnam suggests in the earlier parts
of his book when he mentions law and the courts, that people are
ready to trust others in situations of uncertainty because of their
confidence in institutional sanctions and incentives which are
backed by government? In other words, I trust another person,
even if I am quite ignorant about her character and have no experience of her to draw upon, because I am confident that a
contract between us will be upheld by the law, and that if the
other fails to honour the contract legal sanctions will come into
play. Or I might be willing to trust her because of something
such as a code of professional ethics, which is backed up by a set
of arrangements for professional accreditation. I don't have to
trust her as a person if I am confident about the incentives and
sanctions to which she is subject. Part of the function of institutions is, in a sense, to replace personal knowledge. As Levi says,
'Although it is still an open empirical question, I believe trust is
more likely to emerge in response to experiences and institutions
outside the small associations . . . Expectations about the behaviour of others form as a result of interactions among groups
defined by ethnicity, religion or some other shared value; confidence in a back-drop of third-party sanctions; or sufficient costs
to discourage the betrayal of trust.'[23]

In point of fact there is a lot of evidence that state institutions
can lay the basis for generalized trust (as Putnam seems to have

recognized before he got to chapter 6 of *Making Democracy Work*). This is the subject of a significant exchange between Platteau and Moore. The former – influenced in part by Putnam – argues that for an effective and tolerably efficient market economy it is necessary for there to be a generalized morality in the society (rather than the kind of segmented morality that Saberwal, for example, ascribes to Indian society, and which is identified by others elsewhere – in Russia, for instance, after the collapse of the Soviet Union). It is really a Weberian argument, leaning towards cultural explanation, like Weber's theory of the way in which 'the Protestant Ethic' facilitated the development of capitalism because of the way in which it imbued a spirit of rational calculation. Moore, however, refers to historical research on the United States in the later nineteenth century, showing the possibility of the *production of trust* by institutional innovation, involving the agency of the state, and through such mechanisms as professional certification, and the development of banking, insurance, government and legal services.[24] Deliberate political action can build institutions that promote 'civility'. And, somewhat ironically for the argument of *Making Democracy Work*, recent empirical research by Brehm and Rahm has shown 'a stronger relationship running from trust in institutions to interpersonal trust than the other way round, suggesting that more trustworthy governmental institutions make for greater social trust in a society'.[25]

In reducing the idea of civil society, as he does in chapter 6 of *Making Democracy Work*, to just 'voluntary associations', not taking account of the role of legal institutions or of codes of practice such as professional ethics, or of the importance of people's confidence in them for a sense of 'civicness' to develop, Putnam ends up by misinterpreting his own data. 'His research suggests that well-designed political institutions are crucial to fostering civic spirit because they provide enabling conditions – a political opportunity structure – that could become an incentive to civil actors to emerge and a target of influence for them once they do'.[26] But this is not the interpretative path that Putnam takes.

Margaret Levi's conclusion is emphatic: Putnam 'lacks a theory of social capital'.[27] His metaphorical use of Coleman's idea obscures rather than illuminates. Putnam's usage, as Jean Cohen points out:

allows one to avoid the difficult task of showing that the particular trust built up between specific individuals in one context can be transferred without further ado to other contexts, to strangers, or to society at large. In short, before the issue of what generalizes social capital is the question of whether 'inherited social capital' [what is elsewhere referred to as 'stocks' of norms, networks and trust] is the right concept to use for *six* rather different things: interpersonal trust, social solidarity, general norms of reciprocity, belief in the legitimacy of institutionalised norms [such as laws and codes of professional conduct], confidence that these will motivate the action of institutional actors and ordinary citizens (social solidarity), and the transmission of cultural traditions, patterns and values.[28]

Conclusion

Those of us who are critical of Putnam are certainly not arguing that trust and reciprocity (the ideas/values which are referred to in the concept of 'social capital') are unimportant in relation to cooperation between people, and to functioning democracy. Nor are we suggesting that what Putnam calls 'civic engagement' doesn't matter. There is no need to romanticize 'the Kerala model' – to take one specific historical example – in order to recognize the value of 'public action' (aka 'civic engagement'). But the crucial question is whether the idea of 'social capital' as it has been popularized through Putnam's work doesn't actually confuse and mislead, and in a particular way that has the effect of obscuring the role of politics. Summing up:

1. The idea of social capital' (in general) suggests a false analogy with what is popularly, even if misleadingly, understood to be 'capital' (the 'stuff that produces things'). This can be 'accumulated, saved, inherited and exchanged regardless of its particular form because there is a universal equivalent for it – money'. But interpersonal trust – which is what Putnam, following Coleman, says is an 'essential element' of social capital – is quite clearly not like this. It is by definition specific and contextual. One trusts particular

people, in particular contexts. There is no mechanism whereby such interpersonal trust is generalized. But, clearly, the notion that social relationships can somehow be equated with 'capital' has helped enormously to make the idea of 'social capital' so popular.

2. The metaphorical notion of social capital emerging from Putnam's work (because he has no theory of trust) confuses a number of distinct ideas: interpersonal trust; generalised trust (or 'social solidarity'); belief in the legitimacy of institutionalized norms and confidence in their implementation; and cultural traditions.

3. Treating 'social capital' as referring more or less exclusively to 'horizontal voluntary associations' and what follows from them, as Putnam does at the end of *Making Democracy Work*, eliminates the role of state-backed institutions in creating conditions for the kind of wider civic involvement that is implied in his idea of 'civic engagement'.[29] It implies a highly reductionist view of what constitutes civil society. Without such institutions 'there is no reason to expect that the forms of trust or reciprocity generated within small groups would extend beyond the group or, for that matter, that group demands would be anything other than particularistic'.[30] It is actually very hard to understand how values of impartiality or indeed the idea of a 'citizen' could emerge in such a context.

4. Somewhat ironically Putnam's own account of the history of Italy – flawed though it is in a number of ways, especially because of his ill-considered notion of historical path dependence – hints at another interpretation which suggests that political institutions *are* essential to fostering 'civic spirit'/ 'civic involvement'/ 'civic engagement'. But he is led away from this interpretation by a model that is society-centred and privileges the role of 'horizontal voluntary associations'. Yet the evidence for an alternative historiography showing that state-building, state structures and political processes are essential in accounting both for variations in civic engagement across Italy, and for some of what Putnam holds to be the consequences of this 'engagement', is strong.

So of what possible value is the idea of social capital? As I have suggested already and will proceed to document further, its value lies precisely in the fact that social capital *à la* Putnam, because it asserts the determining consequences of 'voluntary association', obscures the role of state institutions and of politics. The conception of social capital which does seem to make good *analytical* sense is actually that proposed first of all – by Bourdieu. He, it will be recalled, shows how 'durable social relationships' may give rise to differential access to resources. They are an instrument of power and an aspect of class differentiation.

It is precisely this critical understanding of 'social capital' that is overlaid by the kind of romanticism evident in Putnam's work. His view of associational life summons up a romanticized image of 'community' in terms of harmonious sociability, one that is not touched by the kinds of power differences with which Bourdieu is concerned. 'By themselves [too], dense networks support localism, which is often extremely resistant to change', and exclusivism. So 'although his intention is to promote political and economic progress, there is a very conservative message implied in much of what Putnam writes'.[31] This conservatism is even more strikingly apparent in Putnam's work on his native America.

4

'Anti-Politics' in America

The Debate about Social Capital and Civil Society in the United States

(or, Another Harvard professor enters the fray)

If Putnam is right, his work suggests the possibility of solving our problems through low-cost association-strengthening local initiatives that don't require higher taxes.[1]

Robert Putnam's application of his concept of social capital in his American work adds to the confusion documented in the last chapter. He seems to want to be all things to all men – and the fact that his work has appealed both to conservative Republicans and to moderate Democrats suggests that he has come quite near to succeeding. While he has said that 'social capital is not a substitute for effective public policy', he also asserts that it is both a 'prerequisite for it and, in part, a consequence of it'.[2] He ends up once again, in *Bowling Alone: the collapse and revival of American community*[3], elevating 'voluntary association' (no matter what this is actually intended for, or what the content of the activities that bring people together) as the cause of differences in 'health, wealth and happiness' amongst Americans. He panders to communitarianism, and evades issues of power (altogether obscuring the problems and possibilities of class politics). Even more clearly than in *Making Democracy Work* this is an exercise in the operation of the anti-politics machine.

Putnam's America: finding back to de Tocqueville

'Bowling Alone' and the withering of social capital?

Not long after the publication of *Making Democracy Work*, Putnam turned his attention to his native United States, applying the particular 'Tocquevillian' perspective which he had explored in the construction of the 'civic community index' for Italian regions. After an initial *tour de terrain* that appeared at about the same time as the Italian book, in 1993,[4] there came another paper two years later, with a title, 'Bowling Alone: America's declining social capital', which established an evocative image of the state of contemporary American society.[5] 'Bowling Alone' seemed to strike a sensitive nerve and to provide 'a coherent theory to explain the dominant emotion in American politics: a feeling that the quality of our society at the everyday level has deteriorated severely'.[6] Putnam showed that although more Americans go bowling now than ever before, far fewer of them participate in teams and bowling leagues (which are likely to establish the kinds of 'weak' horizontal ties that are the base of social capital, according to the suggestions in chapter 6 of *Making Democracy Work*). Between 1980 and 1993 league bowling evidently fell by 40 per cent. This is a metaphor for American civic life in general, for it is not only bowling leagues that are in decline. Many other forms of association, formal and informal, are much weaker now than they were thirty years ago. Fewer people are involved in community groups; fewer citizens turn out to vote; church attendance is down; union membership is declining. Groups ranging from Rotary Clubs to the Scouts have lost members. Overall, according to the evidence that Putnam had unearthed, there had been a decline of about 25 per cent in membership in voluntary associations since the 1970s.

In the essay on 'Bowling Alone', and then in greater depth in 'The strange disappearance of civic America',[7] Putnam analysed the causes of the decline in the kinds of associations that de Tocqueville had believed to be such a distinctive and important feature of American democracy (not just, or even particularly political associations, remember). His conclusion was that there is a strong generational effect, and that those born in the period between about 1910 and 1940 (he later specified in particular the cohort born between 1925 and 1930) are more likely to participate in or to have participated in associations than those born afterwards; and that the principal cause of this generational change is probably the effect of television, which has individualized the way in which people spend their leisure time: 'each hour spent viewing television is associated with less social trust and less group membership'.[8] These in turn are supposed to have contributed significantly to the weakening of American democracy.

'Bunk' or conservative propaganda?

These papers gave rise to vigorous debate.[9] While Putnam's arguments were widely appreciated by politicians, both Republicans and Democrats, who found in them support, variously, for cutting back on government expenditure and relying on the private sector and voluntary organizations, or for programmes intended to rebuild communities, another response was reflected in the title of an article in *The Washington Post*: 'The "bowling alone" phenomenon is bunk'. Robert Samuelson, the author of this piece, questioned Putnam's statistics, pointing out that the 25 per cent decline of all group membership since 1974 that Putnam so emphasized occurs 'only after he makes a statistical adjustment for rising educational levels. In the past, better-educated people have belonged to more groups. Because group joining hasn't risen with rising schooling, Putnam finds a startling "decline".'[10] Discounting the adjustment, the evidence doesn't suggest a lot of change; moreover, there are indications from other sources of positive movements, like the increase that has taken place in volunteering. 'The whole theory', Samuelson decides, 'is dubious. It aims to explain a 'loss of community': a growing feeling of social splintering. Whether this is real or not is unclear. Since World War II just when has America been one big happy family? Perhaps, briefly, in the mid-1950s between McCarthyism and, later, Sputnik and school desegregation crises.' Other commentators, too, remarked upon the kind of romantic nostalgia for the 1950s reflected in 'Bowling Alone', which overlooks both the extent of prejudice and of social divisions in the United States at that time, and the extent to which the kinds of associations that were strong were the preserve, very largely, of older white men, or of women as housewives.

Lemann's 'Kicking in Groups' (a reference to the rapid growth in US Youth Soccer over the period of the decline of the bowling leagues) – cited in the quotation at the head of this chapter – is a more considered statement on the same lines. This writer also makes the important point that Putnam changed his tune in a remarkable way when he turned his attention from Italy to the United States. 'Civic engagement' in Italy, remember, is subject to 'historical path dependence'. The vibrancy of associational life in north-central Italy, and the supposed lack of it in the South, are held to be the outcome of long-term historical processes, and difficult to change. Yet it seems that in the United States it is possible for there to have been an extraordinary decline in associational life over a very short period; in his practical conclusions Putnam implies that active citizens (such as himself) can turn things around again in a similarly short period of time. Contrast this with the conclusion of *Making Democracy Work*, that I cited earlier: 'most institutional history moves slowly'. But if there are glaciers in Italy there seem, by contrast, to be only fast-flowing streams in the United States. The point is that which I raised in chapter 2 and then examined in some depth in chapter 3 – concerning Putnam's strange notions of the relations between structure and agency.

Most crucially, perhaps, there is the possibility that what has been happening in America is not so much the decline of civic community as its mutation: 'Bowling leagues, Elks and Lions, and the League of Women Voters are indisputably not what they used to be. These forms of association that are culturally connected to older cities and to old-fashioned gender roles (bowling leagues are a good example) [have atrophied] while other forms more oriented to open space and to weekends (like youth soccer) have grown.'[11] The last thirty years have seen various trends in American civil society, some of them contradictory. There has been, therefore, 'a complex historical dynamic in which substantial learning and capacity building has taken place amidst many broader indicators of decline [so that] . . . The capacit[ies] of community-based organizations to engage in complex public–private partnerships are far greater than in the 1960s, and have been increasing steadily.'[12] The decline of forms of social capital such as bowling leagues, or those which were downright illiberal and social-exclusivist, may not matter all that much, then, beside the development of new forms of community problem-solving (though it is true, Sirianni and Friedland note, that church attendance has been declining, which is significant for the sorts of community action which interest them).

Of particular interest in view of Putnam's argument about the direction of causality in the relationships between 'civic engagement' and government performance in Italy, as well as of his views on the decline of social capital in America, is the finding that 'Federal support for Community Action [a programme of the Johnson administration in the 1960s] and a variety of other programmes that grew up around it, was a very important factor in spurring the development of new forms of social capital . . . Community Action turned out to be a vast incubator for involving new community actors . . . building local associations, forging broader networks, and laying the foundations for new forms of collaboration between local groups and city and service agencies'.[13] Sirianni and Friedland refer to the possibility of mutually supportive relationships (synergy[14]) between state and civic action. Putnam acknowledges this possibility, too, but it is overlaid by the emphasis that he places on civic organization as taking place in a realm of its own. And it is this which has made what he writes – in spite of his own avowed political sympathies – so attractive to conservative politicians like Senator Dan Coats, one of the founders of the 'Project of American Renewal', which was an ambitious programme for cutting back the role of the state and (for example) shifting responsibilities for welfare to 'private and religious charities'.[15]

Skocpol: on not treating social capital as a realm apart

The ambivalence in Putnam's arguments about social capital in America, which made his ideas so attractive to the political right, was commented upon by one of the most powerful of his academic critics: his Harvard colleague, Professor Theda Skocpol. She too noted how 'many conservatives are rallying around this notion of civil society as an alternative to extra-local government' and then commented with approval upon Senator Bill Bradley's contrary declaration in 1995 that 'Too often those who trash government as the enemy of freedom and a destroyer of families are strangely silent about the market's corrosive effects on those very same values in civil society'.[16] But she actually accepted – 'despite qualms about the data' – Putnam's broad findings and agreed that he 'put his finger on a historic break in US associational life'. Her own researches, however, on civic life in the United States[17] led her to some significantly different conclusions from those described by Putnam. Whereas, according to his account, associational life is predominantly local and the outcome of individual initiatives – Skocpol comments that 'Ironically for a scholar who calls for attention to social interconnectedness, Putnam works with atomistic concepts and data' – Skocpol found that 'US civic associations were encouraged by the American Revolution, the Civil War, the New Deal, and World Wars I and II; and until recently they were fostered by the institutional patterns of US federalism, legislatures, competitive elections, and locally rooted political parties.' Her key point – grounded in her own substantive historical analysis of 'How Americans Became Civic' – is that *Putnam is wrong to suppose, as he often seems to, 'that social capital is something that arises or declines in a realm apart from politics and government'* (emphasis added). This is exactly the criticism that Tarrow also makes in regard to the arguments about Italy in *Making Democracy Work*.

Skocpol's findings are that, whereas popular wisdom – clearly reflected in Putnam's writings – has it that voluntary groups flourished in the United States because there was no strong national state, and that they had, therefore, very much of a 'local' character, on the contrary these groups were often built 'from the top down':

> From the very beginning of the American nation, democratic governmental and political institutions encouraged the proliferation of voluntary groups linked to regional or national social movements and, increasingly, also tied into translocal organizational networks that paralleled the local-national structure of the US state. Moral-reform movements; farmers' and workers' associations; fraternal brotherhoods devoted to ritual, mutual aid and service; independent women's associations; veterans' groups; and many ethnic and African-American associations – all converged on this quintessentially American form of voluntary association. Local face-to-face participation complemented and went along with organized routes into county, state, regional and national public affairs.[18]

The federal state also encouraged voluntary associations indirectly, for example, by its contribution to the communications infrastructure. By 1828, according to one study of the US Postal Service, 'the American postal system had almost twice as many offices as the postal system in Great Britain and over five times as many offices as the postal system in France'.[19] On the other hand many of the federal programmes of social expenditure that are so decried now by conservatives, who want to 'roll back the state' and replace it with voluntary organizations and the private sector, were actually initiated as a result of pressure from voluntary membership associations. Throughout, they 'have complemented the US version of the modern welfare state'.

Another historian who has studied associations in nineteenth-century America, Mary P Ryan, adds another element to this questioning of the centrality of voluntary association in the building of democracy in America, reminding us that the notion that 'voluntary association' is more or less synonymous with 'civil society' is highly misleading. Ryan accepts that 'social capital' is an apt metaphor for the associations in the cities she studied:

> But measurements of social capital cannot [she says] capture the vitality of democratic politics in America. Civic engagement flourished: it was passionate, contentious, and not always civil. Nor did it always depend on voluntary associations . . . [which] rarely created social meaning in the way that social movements focusing on single issues, or sets of issues, did. More complex than social capital, the combination of associations, public meetings, political parties and social movements had, by mid-century, empowered citizens and helped support the growth of democracy.[20]

There are strong reasons, therefore, for doubting the directions of causality in Putnam's argument. Skocpol suggests, too, that at least as good as the evidence for Putnam's 'TV-watching' explanation for the decline in associational loyalties is the evidence for the hypothesis that it has come about as a result of the shifting allegiances of the elite. The burgeoning numbers of well-educated and highly paid executives, managers and professionals may well have pulled out of locally rooted civic associations. Rather than finding in local associations stepping stones for their ambitions and convenient vehicles for the pursuit of their interests, it seems that now they feel that they do better by devoting their energies to their work and pursuing their interests through national lobbying organizations based in Washington. And, says Skocpol, expressing very clearly the concern which has also run through my discussion of Putnam's work:

> How ironic it would be if, after pulling out of locally rooted associations, the very business and professional elites who blazed the path toward local civic disengagement were now to turn around and successfully argue that the less privileged Americans they left behind are the ones who must repair the nation's social connectedness, by pulling themselves together from below without much help from government or their privileged fellow citizens. This, I fear, is what is happening as the discussion about 'returning to de Tocqueville' rages across elite America.[21]

'Bowling Alone' again, and social capital on its own once more

Whereas Putnam has never responded to criticisms of *Making Democracy Work* (which I explained in the last chapter), 'Bowling Alone' has grown into a book, *Bowling Alone: the collapse and revival of American community*,[22] in which he does claim to respond to the critics of his American work. It has to be said, however, that a favourite Putnam tactic is to acknowledge criticisms graciously, in the manner of the New England gentleman, without paying the slightest bit of attention to them. The new *Bowling Alone* is consequently largely a 'restatement', not a 'revised statement', providing massive statistical documentation of the argument of the earlier article.

Reading *Bowling Alone*, said a reviewer in *The Washington Post*, is 'like sipping sociology from a fire hose'. Drawing in particular on the results of regularly repeated surveys on social and political trends, on panel data constructed in repeated surveys conducted by an advertising agency, and on the results of a University of Maryland project in which samples of Americans kept time diaries in 1965, 1975, 1985 and 1995, the book seems massively to justify the claims Putnam made earlier. The decline of organized league bowling does appear to be an apt metaphor of the very widespread decline in participation by Americans of all statuses, races and religions, in political, civic, religious and work organizations since the high point of such 'civic engagement' in the 1960s; and of the decline, too, since that time, in all manner of simple forms of everyday socializing, like playing cards together, entertaining family, friends and neighbours at home, or even the commonplace sharing of dinner together by the members of a family. Americans are still more sociable – more willing participants in civic activities and more enthusiastic socializers – than are the members of most other 'developed' societies, but they appear to be much less sociable, both formally and informally, than they were.

One common criticism of Putnam's earlier account of the declining sociability of Americans, as we saw, is that he mistakes the decline of older forms of civic organization, which were dominated by older white men or by women as housewives, for that of all forms of association and sociability. The critics point to the exclusiveness of many of the old, established membership organizations, and to the rise in their place of much more open ways in which people get together. There are new kinds of organizations, they argue, that are both more open and address a whole range of needs, like the American Association of Retired Persons (the AARP – now the largest organization in America, and still growing rapidly) and a congeries of environmental organizations and of civic NGOs. If organizations that depended upon the involvement of women as mothers and housewives have declined as more and more women have entered the workforce, isn't this really a positive development? And aren't women now getting together in different ways both at work and in their leisure? Isn't the workplace, indeed, becoming a more important forum where people are brought together than the residential community? Putnam concedes something to these arguments, and he strives to distance himself from the charge that he is afflicted by a romantic nostalgia for the more organized but also less tolerant and more exclusivist days of the 1940s and 1950s. He surely has a case when he distinguishes between the kinds of organizations which have local chapters and which bring people together face-to-face, and those that have grown latterly. These are mostly associations that encourage 'participation' via the cheque-book – they are about mass-mailing rather than mass movement – and run large bureaucracies to conduct lobbying operations in Washington. They may be effective, but they are not 'membership' organizations in the same sense as, say, the Lions or the Rotary Club. Whether they have the 'Tocqueville effects', internally on individual members and externally on the wider polity, is at least questionable. 'Participation' by citizens as 'disgruntled claimants upon the state' is not quite the same as active participation in local community action.[23] Neither are workplaces, in these times of 'flexible' labour markets, part-time working and insecure employment, really 'communities' except when it suits companies to try to create such an illusion.

Yet Putnam's strong conclusions about 'the collapse of American community' are not entirely proof against the counter-claim that forms of socializing have changed in ways that are not picked up in the surveys on which he relies. It is not just that the 'tavern' or local bar is less important as a meeting place these days than the coffee shop, but more significantly that there are social groupings among the young participants in contemporary youth culture, and among women, reflecting new and different forms of sociability that are not encompassed by the surveys. In the main, the counter-argument runs, Putnam's 'facts' accurately reflect significant social change in America, but whether they show the kind of 'decline in community' that he claims for them is another matter. The exceptions that Putnam himself notes to the general trend that he asserts seem, ironically, to provide some evidence in support of his critics' views. He himself concedes that volunteer activities are up, and one authority on voluntary organizations in the United States holds that 'Our nation has ever been more caring for the previously disadvantaged or excluded, from ethnic and religious minorities to gays, battered women, and children'.[24] The generation in America that Putnam holds responsible for the 'decline of community' has been responsible, too, for having created 'the first consumers' movement since the 1930s, the first environmental movement since the turn of the century, public health movements, grassroots activism and community organizing, the first feminist movement since the pre-World War I period, the civil rights movement, and innumerable transnational nongovernmental organizations and civic movements [like those that took such effective action against the thoroughly antidemocratic WTO at its Seattle meetings in 1999], all of which have led to unprecedented advances in rights and social justice'.[25] This kind of civic activism cannot be dismissed as simply 'mail order' stuff. It draws rather on all sorts of informal groups and networks (increasingly facilitated by the use of the internet or mobile phones[26]) even if it does not draw on nor lend vitality to the older kinds of associations. This hardly all adds up to a picture of 'the collapse of community'. Putnam's image of collapse is an artefact of his method, and he has not defended it convincingly against his critics.

The second part of the book addresses the question, 'Why did the fabric of American community life begin to unravel?' Here earlier arguments are substantiated and refined. The most important factor, it seems, is that of generational change (and Putnam defends himself vigorously against the charge that he placed too much explanatory weight on the effects of the introduction of television). There is 'a long civic generation, born roughly between 1910 and 1940, a broad group of people substantially more engaged in community affairs and more trusting than those younger than they'.[27] A large part of the decline in civic engagement and of sociability is due to the passing of this 'civic generation', whose approach to life seems to have been strongly influenced by its experience of the Great Depression, and then of obligation to the wider community during wartime [a point that reflects Skocpol's arguments about the relationships between major points of crisis in American history and the phenomena of 'joining'], whereas those in the succeeding generations are more inclined to individualistic and materialistic values. The increased pressures on time and money in the 1970s and 1980s, the increased participation of women in the workforce, the consequences of suburbanization, and – probably most important among these other factors – the amount of time which people spend in front of their television sets, have also played a part.

The most interesting and original parts of *Bowling Alone* are the final two sections in which Putnam asks the questions 'So What?' and 'What Is To Be Done?' (about the decline in civic engagement). In the first of these he constructs an index of social capital for the states of the Union, and then shows how (and explains why) social capital – thus measured – is correlated with higher educational levels and better-performing schools, higher levels of health and happiness, more secure environments, and (probably – the arguments here are more speculative) with more efficient economies and democratic government. The measure of social capital is constructed – like that of 'civic community' in *Making Democracy Work* – by combining a number of indices (of 'community organizational life', 'engagement in public affairs', 'community volunteerism', 'informal socializing' and of 'social trust') which are themselves highly intercorrelated. There are substantial differences in the level of the index between the states at the top, which include Nebraska, the Dakotas and Vermont (the 'high-pressure centre' of social capital in America is in the Centre-North and the North West), and those at the bottom (in the 'low-pressure centre' over the Mississippi Delta) – Louisiana, Alabama, Mississippi, Georgia and Tennessee. Putnam notes, but seems then not to reflect upon the possible implications of his observation, that, 'It is not happenstance that the lowest levels of community-based social capital are found where a century of plantation slavery was followed by a century of Jim Crow politics [referring to the disenfranchisement of the Southern blacks in the 1890s]. *Inequality and social solidarity are deeply incompatible* (emphasis added).'[28]

Putnam notes the need for caution in inferring causality from correlations such as those that he shows between his index of social capital and various good things, but having entered this caveat he then proceeds very largely to ignore it. He does note the connections between levels of education and social capital, but not their possible (independent) causal effects when it comes to explaining variations in levels of 'health and happiness' (etc.).[29] Most strangely, given the emphatic statement which I have quoted concerning the inverse relationships between social capital as he defines it and inequality, there is no effort at distinguishing the effects of inequality upon schooling, standards of health care and the like. Putnam is most concerned to demonstrate, in a chapter on the 'dark side' of social capital, that there is no incompatibility between social capital (which might be equated with 'fraternity') and the other Enlightenment values of liberty and equality. He recognizes the possibility that – as Bourdieu, whom he does not cite, showed – 'social capital, particularly social capital that bonds us with others like us, often reinforces social stratification'. But he wants to reassure his readers that *'Community and equality are mutually reinforcing, not mutually incompatible'* (his emphasis). Both over time and across space it can easily be shown that in America equality and social capital move in tandem. He shows that 'high social capital states' are also the states most characterized by economic and civic equality.[30] He also notes the correlation between the period in the 1950s and 1960s when America was more egalitarian than it had been for over a century and the high point of connectedness and of civic engagement; and that, by contrast, 'the last third of the twentieth century was a time of growing inequality *and* eroding social capital'. He goes on to remark that:

> By the end of the twentieth century the gap between rich and poor in the United States had been increasing for nearly three decades, the longest sustained increase in equality in at least a century [some have argued that America is now more inegalitarian than at any time in its history], coupled with the first sustained decline in social capital in at least as long. The timing of the two trends is striking.[31]

It is indeed. Yet it does not enter into Putnam's explanation for why social capital should have declined in the way that it has done (according to his measures) since the 1960s. He can only end, rather lamely, by conceding that his 'simple analysis cannot detect what is causing what here' – which being so, it is surprising that he should be so ready to publish a big book which purports to demonstrate that 'the decline in social capital' is at the root of the present-day ills of American society. A more convincing conclusion concerning the relationships between inequality and community organization is the one reached by Samuel Bowles: 'among US localities, participation in church, local service and political groups, and other community organizations was found to be substantially higher where income was more equally distributed, suggesting that *policies to increase income equality would enhance community governance'* (emphasis added).[32]

Putnam does not think of himself as a conservative and he is keen to show that the decline in social capital in America is not the result of high levels of state expenditure (as American

conservatives, responding to him, have argued). Both in the book
and in an earlier 'reply to critics' he wants, he says, to 'resist the
view, now being articulated by some simple-minded reactionaries
[Senator Coats, cited above, perhaps] that government can be
replaced by "civil society"'; and he pronounces sternly against
'sterile academic debates about "the state" versus "civil society",
for both are plainly important'.[33] But the fact remains that the
impression he gives is that it is 'getting together' that counts. The
last part of his book, on 'What Is To Be Done?' contains a long
and interesting chapter on 'Lessons of History: The Gilded Age
and the Progressive Era', about the end of the nineteenth century
and the early part of the twentieth, a period in American history
in which there appears to have been decline and then revival of
social capital. The analysis, in part, parallels Skocpol's on the
history of civic America. Yet Putnam concludes – contra Skocpol
(though without addressing her arguments, which are cited
above) – that *'investment in social capital was not an alternative to,
but a prerequisite for, political mobilization and reform'* (emphasis in
original).[34] Both writers no doubt recognize an interplay between
organization in civil society and political organization. But
Putnam, here at least, explicitly weights the civil society side of
the equation (much more so, indeed, than he did in his first intervention in 1993. It is hard to avoid the feeling that the runaway
success of the social capital idea has led him to throw caution,
nuance and history out of the window). Yet he goes on to note
that many historians of the Progressive Era have argued that
reform and the organization that came with it were a response to
the perceived 'threat' from the working class.

   Turn then to his prescriptions for 'An Agenda for Social
Capitalists'.[35] I shall not list all his injunctions in this oddly
voluntaristic conclusion to a book which, for all its sometimes
inverted logic, nonetheless does give a structural account of
why there should have been a decline in the sorts of associations
with which it is concerned. A few of Putnam's Commandments
will suffice:

   Let us find ways to ensure that by 2010 the level of civic
   engagement among Americans then coming of age in all
   parts of our society will match that of their grandparents
   when they were at that same age, and that at the same time

bridging capital will be substantially greater than it was in their grandparents' era.

Let us find ways to ensure that by 2010 America's work-places will be substantially more family-friendly and community-congenial . . .

Let us ensure that by 2010 Americans will spend less time travelling and more time connected with our neighbours . . .

Let us find ways to ensure that by 2010 Americans will spend less leisure time sitting passively alone in front of glowing screens . . . [36]

These are worthy wishes, perhaps. But there is no mention here of the deepening inequality in American society, no commentary on how to tackle the crushing burden of poverty which afflicts so many Americans. No mention, either, of the political struggles that will be necessary if those who are excluded from the ample fruits of American prosperity – and who may or who may not be 'socially connected', according to Putnam's own account of them – are to move in (sometimes literally, not just metaphorically) out of the cold. There is surely room to doubt whether the menu that Putnam offers, of improved civic education, more humane urban planning, the renewal of the Scout movement and the like, will really do the trick.

Bowling Alone has been likened to other great and influential studies of American society. One of these is Gunnar Myrdal's vast work, published in 1944, on *An American Dilemma: The Negro Problem and American Democracy*. Myrdal was quite centrally concerned with the problem posed by the fact that Americans do not live up to their beliefs, a 'Creed' which, he argued in his exposition of it, holds that no group in America should be allowed to fall below a certain minimum level of living, and that all groups and individuals should have equal opportunity. *American Dilemma* documented in detail just how far the America of the mid-twentieth century departed from these ideals. How much further has America now moved away from these values, given the deepening inequality in American society, in which 20 per cent of children now live in poverty (putting the United States, in this unfortunate respect, in 'first place among industrial nations'). Myrdal also showed how Americans defended their Creed from its shortcomings, sometimes through practices in which social scientists played no small part: 'American social science overstated its objective neutrality and defended the American Creed against its apparent contradictions by attributing the cause of inequality to some group, individual or genetic condition [such as in the notion of 'the culture of poverty'] . . . inequalities and their remedies were not the products of social relationships and thus were not subjects for social or public remedy.'[37] Ironically, given his concern with social relationships, this seems nonetheless a fitting commentary on the work of Robert Putnam on his native America. 'Social capital', in his account of it, takes on a life of its own. It is attributed with causal significance which cannot be justified. And it finally veils the roots of inequality. In its own way Putnam's social capital constitutes another anti-politics machine.

Conclusion

Putnam's work on America, after the initial stimulus from *Making Democracy Work*, has given currency to the idea that 'social capital' in some way holds the key to the resolution of all sorts of social problems. His observation that Americans now 'bowl alone', rather than in teams, is a powerful metaphor for the decline in certain kinds of formal and informal associations in America, and hence for what is widely felt to be 'the collapse of American community'. Quite apart from the methodological problems associated with this work, and the extent to which Putnam's interpretations seem to have been influenced – his protestations to the contrary notwithstanding – by a nostalgic view of mid-twentieth-century America (which was actually more racist, exclusivist and intolerant than it is today), the major flaw within it – recalling the logical flaws of chapter 6 of *Making Democracy Work* – has to do with the way in which 'social capital' is set in a realm apart from politics and government. One consequence of this is that 'social capital' is attributed with a causal significance that is logically and empirically unjustified. Putnam is unwilling to contemplate a possible implication of his observation that social capital and inequality are antithetical to one another. This is the implication that what matters most in late-twentieth-century America is that inequality is greater than it has been for a very long time, perhaps ever, and that a high proportion of Americans live in poverty. His prescriptions, which refer not at all to these material conditions, show at last how the idea of social capital has lent itself so well to the project of depoliticization.

5

Social Capital and 'Synergy across the Public–Private Divide'

(or, A California professor comes to the rescue?)

Social capital inheres, not just in civil society, but in an enduring set of relationships that spans the public–private divide.

Peter Evans[1]

(A) high degree of associationalism in and of itself cannot explain the structural transformations that have underscored Kerala's social development. The redistributive thrust of Kerala's development has carried with it a direct attack on traditional structures of power [and entails] a fundamental realignment in the balance of class forces.

Patrick Heller[2]

This chapter takes up the most significant body of work on social capital since the publication of *Making Democracy Work*. It is a collection of research studies, all by scholars working in American universities and brought together by Peter Evans, a professor of sociology at the University of California, Berkeley,[3] and some subsequent studies by the same group. Each of the individual studies, and Evans' own careful and insightful constructions upon them, acknowledges the influence of Putnam's work. Yet a close reading of them shows their authors to be distinctly uncomfortable with the concept of social capital as he has elaborated it. Evans himself and his co-workers not only 'bring the state back in' but also recognize the salience of politics – and in doing so they are more critical of Putnam than most of them directly acknowledge. Whether because of academic courtesy or – more likely – the prevailing intellectual and political climate in the United States, with its inherent mistrust of left-wing politics, they seem in the end to attempt the rescue of the idea of social capital from its critics. I shall argue that they rather complete its dispatch. In doing so they have also created some difficulties for those in the World Bank and elsewhere who want to take over the neat notion of social capital – meaning 'horizontal/voluntary/local association' – as constituting the 'missing link' in development. This is a theme which I shall take up in chapter 6.

The core of the case put by Peter Evans lies in the statement that heads this chapter: social capital inheres rather in relationships that span 'the public–private divide' than in civil society on its own. Quite contrary to the ideas that Putnam finally emphasizes in both his Italian and in his American odysseys, the 'Evans group' finds that prior endowments of social capital (accumulated perhaps over several centuries) are *not* the crucial factor in creating the virtuous circle (or 'synergy') in which 'civic engagement' nurtures good government and good government in turn fosters civic engagement. The possibilities for such synergy are constrained:

> less by the initial density of trust and ties at the micro-level and more by the difficulties involved in 'scaling-up' micro-level social capital to generate solidary ties and social action on a scale that is politically and economically efficacious . . . Ties among friends and neighbours based in trust and rooted in everyday interactions are essential foundations [but] the key point is that such ties seem to be a resource that is available to most Third World [*sic*] communities . . . [so that] if synergy fails to occur, it is probably not because the relevant neighbourhoods and communities were too fissiporous and mistrustful but because some other crucial ingredient was lacking.[4]

These 'ingredients', it is suggested, are the presence of 'coherent, dependable public [that is, bureaucratic] institutions', and a favourable political regime, characterized by political competition that is 'constrained by mutually accepted ground rules', in a context of a 'relatively egalitarian social structure'.

Evans concludes, therefore, that 'looking at the political and social structural factors associated with synergy is somewhat discouraging. If egalitarian societies with robust public bureaucracies provide the most fertile ground for synergistic state–society relations, most of the Third World offers arid prospects'. So, he says, 'Having begun by rejecting the pessimistic proposition that only areas with exceptional endowments of social capital would be able to enjoy the benefits of synergy [the position adopted by Putnam in *Making Democracy Work*], I seem to have fallen into an equally pessimistic appraisal based on a different set of arguments.' And though he goes on to attempt to argue against such pessimism he still concludes that, while there may be possibilities of achieving small-scale successes in divided societies without strong public institutions, 'it would be foolish to ignore adverse sociopolitical circumstances'.[5] Any suggestion, therefore, that the idea of social capital offers a magic bullet, or the 'missing link' in development, is quashed in Evans' arguments – precisely because he and his fellow researchers take account of wider socio-political contexts in a way that Putnam and his followers do not.

Two aspects of synergy: 'complementarity' and 'embeddedness'

The research studies on which Evans bases his general arguments refer to the relationships between bureaucrats and farmers in Taiwanese irrigation systems, to the relations between a highly mobilized industrial workforce in Kerala and the government, to instances of 'co-production' involving the joint activity of citizens and government, the relations of state and peasant organizations in Mexico, state and industry in post-reform Russia, and to various instances of governmental reform in northeast Brazil.[6] In subsequent work with other colleagues he has studied what he calls 'struggles for livability' in a number of cities in different parts of Asia and Latin America, in which he examines the nexus of relationships among communities, social movement organizations, political parties, NGOs and local government agencies.[7] All of this work concerns the relationships between state agencies and people who are, more or less, organized in society outside the state, and it asks what sorts of arrangements make for the best results for people and for society in general.

Contrary both to those neo-liberal arguments advocating the minimization of the role of the state (so that markets can function 'freely'), and to interpretations of Putnam's work that stress the primary importance of organization in 'civil society', Evans and his co-workers show that there is complementarity in the relationship between state agencies and people. An elementary illustration of this comes from large-scale canal irrigation systems. While it is usually true that farmers can manage the allocation and distribution of water at the local level much more effectively than bureaucrats from an irrigation department who don't have the same levels of knowledge or motivation, it is difficult for local (participatory) 'users'-groups' either to construct or to manage the large-scale works on which local systems depend. These tasks are most efficiently handled by a bureaucratic organization. For local management of irrigation to work well local users need to be able to depend upon the delivery of water to them along the main distributory canals. If there are high levels of uncertainty, and especially if there is conflict over access to water in the first place, then it is rather unlikely that collective action at the local level will even be forthcoming, let alone be successful. There is a division of labour. State/bureaucratic organization at one level and management through participatory groups locally *complement* each other. The better the state agency functions, the better the local association is likely to function, and vice versa (because just as predictable delivery of water is a condition for successful management by local users, so the existence of functioning users' groups is likely to keep the bureaucrats on their toes: in other words, there is 'synergy' between these levels).[8]

Research on irrigation management also shows up another aspect of the relationships between state agencies and society ('across the public–private divide', in other words). While it has usually been held that relationships crossing the divide, between citizens and individual bureaucrats, are likely to have perverse effects on development because they are associated with corruption (as is the case if some farmers are able to bribe irrigation officials to secure preferential access to water), there are also cases which show that the 'embeddedness' of public servants in wider social relationships can have very positive effects. In India it has generally been the case that local-level bureaucrats, such as irrigation officials, are not posted to their own home areas, and it has also been a general principle that officials should be transferred regularly, precisely in order to avoid the possibility that they develop close relationships with any of those whom they are supposed to serve. This approach goes back to the colonial period, when it clearly was intended to facilitate the colonialists' control over the lower echelons of the bureaucracy. In Taiwanese irrigation management, however – and the same is broadly true elsewhere in East Asia – exactly the reverse reasoning is applied, with, it seems, very positive consequences for the efficiency of water use. According to Moore, 'Irrigation associations are over-whelmingly staffed by people who were born in the locality, have lived there all their lives, and in many cases also farm there . . . [so that] . . . IA staff are so much part of the local society that they can neither escape uncomfortable censure if they are seen to be conspicuously performing poorly, nor ignore representations made to them by members.'[9] In other words, 'embeddedness' of officials in society – though in conditions in which their interac-tions with people are subject to rules that ensure proper conduct – can contribute to creating synergy between state and citizens' action. Officials depend for their success upon their rela-tionships with the people they are supposed to serve, just as the people depend upon them for success in their enterprises. The existence of relatively egalitarian social relations is probably another aspect of the story from Taiwan, however – and is one to which Evans returns (as shall we).

These examples from the field of irrigation serve to introduce and to illustrate general arguments. Just as bureaucratic action in the irrigation case contributes to creating synergy across the public–private divide by establishing a predictable environment, so in general a critical role that states play is the provision of a 'rule-governed environment'. There is complementarity between the establishment of such an environment by the state, and the entrepreneurial activity of individuals in society. Moreover, as Evans points out – drawing on work by Heller on Kerala and Fox on Mexico – the establishment of the rule of universalistic law and the protection of their rights (to assemble, to associate, to express themselves) by the state is perhaps even more important as a condition for the organization of poor and less privileged groups in society. Embeddedness, too, is of much more general significance than in relation to the provision of services to the common people. Significantly – according to Evans' earlier research[10] – it also accounts in great part for the success of industrial development in East Asia. Evans' comparative analysis of the development of the electronics industry in South Korea, India and Brazil suggests that the former's greater success stems from the fact that state officials in South Korea are both protected from the influence of private business people, and are also 'embedded' in close relationships with them (there are, Evans states, 'dense networks of ties that connect state agencies and private capital'). In this way, they are well informed and responsive, just like the low-level irrigation officials in the Taiwanese irrigation systems. In the Indian case Evans found, by contrast, that although senior bureaucrats may have a good degree of autonomy (the 'steel frame' of the Indian Administrative Service retains at least some coherence), policy networks that would 'allow industry experts from within the state apparatus to collect and disseminate information, build consensus, tutor and cajole are missing'.[11] In other words, state officials are insufficiently 'embedded', and they are not engaged in the same way as are those in South Korea, in a *joint project* of industrial transformation with private industry.[12]

'Complementarity' and 'embeddedness' are themselves complementary, and both contribute to the creation of synergy across the public–private divide. The arguments are illustrated perhaps most persuasively in Judith Tendler's studies of government in the state of Ceara in northeast Brazil which, from being one of the Brazilian states with the poorest records of all in relation to human development criteria, was turned around in a remarkably short space of time under the aegis of two young reformist governors (who 'in the process of [political] competition saw pro-poor policies as a way of achieving popularity'). Tendler's focus is on what made for the greatly improved performance of government that was essential for these achievements.[13]

The Ceara story involves a transformation – not universally, or without resistance – in the performance of government employees. Where programmes have been made to work much more effectively than before – in the health sector, in agriculture and in drought relief – it has substantially been because of changes in work organization and in the commitment of government workers. In many ways their patterns of work have come to resemble those associated with the most successful private-sector enterprises: flexible, involving team-work, and a client-centred, problem-solving approach (rather than the delivery of centrally determined 'products'). These in turn have been made possible partly through the creation by the state of an imagery of 'calling' around public service, by means of the complementary provision of an intangible collective good – media publicity. The public celebration of the achievements of public employees (and, it has to be said, the protection of dedicated and capable workers from others who have remained entrenched in the old rent-seeking ways) has helped to create an idea of 'calling'. This same publicity has become, also, an instrument for the monitoring of the performance of the workers (it was 'the flip side of the same messages that made these workers feel recognized and honoured by citizens'). It has shown the public what should be expected of public employees, and publicity has been given, too, to the importance of complaints from members of the public about failures of performance.

Has all this happened because of 'decentralization and participation', drawing on local endowments of social capital, as Putnam's work would have us believe? His conclusions seem to show, after all, that good performance of local government in Italy is conditioned particularly by the existence of a robust civil society with abundant resources of 'social capital'. According to this thinking, 'civil society', when it involves rich resources of social capital, works a certain 'magic' – improving government performance through higher levels of accountability – and it works best at the local level, which is why decentralization is held to be such a good thing.

Tendler's analysis falsifies these propositions. She finds that the improved performance of government workers has rather involved a three-way dynamic between local government, civil society and an active central (that is, state) government. Most strikingly, central government actually took some powers *away* from municipal governments in order, paradoxically, to strengthen local government (the Ceara story illustrates, therefore, 'the ironic paradox of decentralization', which is that, in the words of a former Colombian minister, 'it demands more centralization and more sophisticated political skills at the national level'). The success of the health sector programme, for example, depended in part upon the fact that the central government took away powers of making appointments of local health workers from mayors, forbidding them from undertaking such tasks as the distribution of political campaign leaflets. In other words these primary health care workers were no longer the more-or-less dependent clients of local power-holders. Instead, as local people themselves, 'embedded' in their communities, they could be responsive to local needs:

> Creating new ties between 7,000 newly hired health agents and their communities was the key to the health pro-gramme's success. Starting out in a civic climate in which people were reluctant even to open their doors to anyone working for the government, the new health agents made building relationships of trust between themselves and their 'clients' a central part of their jobs.[14]

Evans concludes:

> In Tendler's description of Ceara's health campaign [as in the account of irrigation in Taiwan, above] social capital is formed by making some who are part of the state apparatus more thoroughly part of the communities in which they work. The networks of trust and collaboration that are cre-ated span the public/private boundary and bind state and civil society together.

This leads him to put the proposition with which this chapter begins, that 'Social capital inheres, not just in civil society, but in an enduring set of relationships that spans the public–private divide'.[15]

The key question then is: in what circumstances does such 'synergy', based on relationships of complementarity and embed-dedness between state and society, arise?

Conditions for synergy

In addressing this question Peter Evans actually contradicts him-self, for he starts off by saying – implicitly agreeing with Putnam – that endowments of social capital *are* critical for the development of synergy. But he promptly goes on to make the statement that I quoted above, that 'limits seem to be set less by the initial density of trust and ties at the micro-level and more by the difficulties involved in "scaling up" micro-level social capital'.[16] There is for example no evidence to suggest that community ties in Taiwan, where irrigation systems work well, drawing on local collective action, are stronger than in Nepal, or Sri Lanka, or elsewhere, where such collective action occurs only rarely. Ceara in northeast Brazil is not known as 'an exceptional repository of civic engagement'. Further – and reinforcing the point – it is far from clear that all strong community ties are necessarily socially beneficial. Evans cites work on Kerala by Patrick Heller, who argues that the natural outcome of a 'vigorous civil society rooted in interests bounded by parochial loyalties' is not 'development', but rather the kind of 'demand overload' which has had such crippling implications for India's economy:[17] 'Traditional associations based on caste and community ties could never have produced the kind of developmental transformation that Kerala has experienced'.[18] Not all forms of collective action are conducive to developmentally useful forms of state intervention (some reveal what has been called the 'dark face' of social capital: see chapters 1 and 6). Heller shows that what has been distinctive about social mobilization in Kerala is its class character. As he says, 'insofar as interests and social resources have been mobilized primarily along class lines, a democratically accountable state and a mobilized society have become organizationally and functionally linked in a manner conducive to the transformative projects broadly associated with development, particularly those of a redistributive character'.[19]

The point is not that social ties and local association are unimportant but rather that they constitute a resource 'that is at least latently available to most Third World communities', so that if synergy fails to occur it would seem that 'something else' is missing. One factor is certainly the existence of 'coherent, dependable public institutions'. The embeddedness of public officials in social networks crossing the public–private divide, both in Taiwanese irrigation systems and in the electronics industry in South Korea, has positive effects in both cases only because the opportunities for corruption and rent-seeking that are so clearly available 'are constrained by powerful internal [bureaucratic] norms and a dependably rewarding system of long-term career benefits'. A great deal depends on the attitude of public-sector workers to people they are supposedly serving – as Tendler's research in Ceara shows up so well. And this depends in turn, as her work also demonstrates, not only on administrative structures but also on the political context. The Ceara story would not have worked out in the way that it did had there not been political competition (after the reinitiation of democratic elections in Brazil), and a motivation for leaders who were trying to challenge the old political elite to intervene in local politics in the way that I described above, and to build connections among subordinate groups. Yet, Evans notes, 'politics and interests often get relegated to the background in discussions of social capital' – which is one of the key, critical points raised in this book about the influential work of Robert Putnam. This criticism of Putnam is implicit in Evans' discussion, too.

The existence of political competition is one factor influencing the possibility of synergy. 'Political competeiveness is useful first of all because it contributes to a climate in which citizens count.' In the Kerala case, as well as in Ceara, it has been extremely important in 'sustaining the commitment of parties (whether in or out of government) to mobilization and the construction of encompassing organizations among subordinate groups'. And even in the context of one-party rule in Taiwan it appears from Lam's account that competition between political factions at the local level 'helps to generate pressure on the Irrigation Associations to remain responsive to the interests of local communities'. Of course it is important, too, that political competition is carried on according to mutually agreed ground rules (not the case in Mexico, according to Fox's account of it, because increased competitiveness there is liable to give rise to repressive action on the part of elites), and that there is an adequate bureaucratic infrastructure as well. 'Post-Soviet Russia allows more political competition than China, but the ineffectual Russian state provides no dependable vehicle to "deliver the goods".'

The nature of political competition is influenced, of course, both by the context of social norms and by underlying social conflicts. The cases which Evans reviews show up very clearly that *relative social equality* is a great advantage both in relation to the creation of social capital (à la Putnam, and just as Putnam himself shows) and to the establishment of 'synergy'. Rural Taiwanese society is one of the most egalitarian – perhaps the most egalitarian – in the world. Building local collective action in such a context, or establishing the advantages of an embedded bureaucracy, are quite different propositions from the circumstances, say, of rural Mexico, 'where large landowners dominate an excluded peasantry', or in those of rural Uttar Pradesh by comparison with Kerala. 'In most Third World countries, the interests of the privileged intrude fundamentally on relations between the state and less privileged groups'; and they make for clientelistic capture by elites of public–private ties. Thus it is that Peter Evans reaches the 'pessimistic' conclusions about the prospects for social-capital-as-synergy that I recorded earlier.

He goes on, however, to argue that synergy is 'constructable'. 'Creative organizational innovations can still produce results,' he suggests, and he refers again to Tendler's Ceara work as showing how the '"soft technologies" of organizational design can have large spill-over effects'. Indeed one can see that some of the aspects of organizational design in Ceara, like the use of media publicity, might well be transferable to other contexts. But even the Ceara case brings out the importance of politics. Had it not been for political conditions that led state leaders to intervene in the way they did in local politics, how effective would the 'soft technologies' have been? In other circumstances, in which leadership at the centre depends directly upon the support of those who hold local power, it is hard to imagine that the use of the media, for example, would have the effects that Tendler describes. Many others, though not Evans himself, have become great believers in the notion that decentralization of government will have the effect of creating what Evans describes as 'synergy', because it will make for government which is both much better informed and more accountable to local people. There is indeed a kind of 'decentralization fever' on the loose in the leading development agencies.[20] The conclusion of Tendler's work is to cast a great deal of doubt on such bland optimism, because it shows up very clearly the paradox that creating more effective government at local level may actually involve the extension of the role of central government in some crucial respects. In Ceara it was to reduce the influence of local power-holders who would otherwise have used decentralized local government as vehicles of their interests. Richard Crook and Alan Sverrisson have reached similar conclusions in a recent, thorough-going review of evidence concerning experiments with decentralization in a number of countries. Where it can be shown that decentralization has been effective both in deepening democracy and in promoting poverty alleviating development (notably in the Indian state of West Bengal, the most successful case that they were able to identify), it is in circumstances in which the interests of poorer people are supported from outside: 'We would emphasize the overriding significance of the politics of local–central relations . . . as the major determinant of the differences between the successful and unsuccessful cases . . . Accountability and responsiveness to the poor is still most likely to emerge locally where representation of their interests can be supported externally, in the context of a conflict between local and central forces with different power bases.'[21] Organizational tinkering can of course have powerful effects but not in isolation from the political context.

Peter Evans' other suggestions about the constructability of synergy are subject to similar reservations. 'The first cornerstone of constructability is that social structures depend upon people's perceptions of themselves and their neighbours and these perceptions are malleable.' Well, quite so. One of the examples he gives comes from Heller's work on Kerala, showing how members of particular castes and religious communities have come to see themselves as members of a working class and hence have been enabled to struggle effectively against landlordism and patron–client relations. These changed perceptions only came about, however, as a result of political activity. Much the same point may be made about Evans' other suggestion, which is that 'constructing synergy can begin with simple redefinition of problems'. This too is a political process; and redefinition of problems is likely to be a process of contestation.

In more recent work, a series of comparative studies in cities of six countries in Asia and Latin America (plus Hungary), Evans and several research associates have shown again that the capacity for collective action (in pursuit of sustainable livelihoods or 'livability') in a community of people is not (as Putnam wrongly concluded that his Italian work showed) a matter of historical endowment, but can be constructed, even in unlikely communities. One condition for the construction of this capacity is that the achievement of some common end should appear to be a feasible possibility, but it also depends on the social and political context of a community. The point is that, while the energy for change may lie within the community, it has to be complemented 'by broader sets of ideas and organization'. External linkages, which may operate through NGOs, social movement organizations, political parties, or even informal connections through individuals with bases outside the community, 'play an essential role in enabling communities to become effective agents of livability. *Romantic visions in which individual communities can somehow resolve problems of livelihood and sustainability on their own are politically misguided and a political disservice* (emphasis added).' Here the role of political parties is decribed as being 'both more ubiquitous and much more complex' than those of the other agents which may be involved. However, we are told that:

> Suggesting that parties are the solution to communities' needs for external linkages would be foolish. Control, clientelism and co-optation and the quest for partisan advantage play much too large a role in the repertoires of even progressive parties. Nevertheless, it would be equally foolish for activists and community leaders to ignore the possibilities that party structures afford and the way that oppositional parties can open up the larger political environment for new discourses and new forms of participation.

To underline this point about the centrality of political action Evans and his co-researchers also find that 'allies within the state are crucial resources for communities and other social groups' – as was also the case in Ceara according to Tendler's account – especially when communities mobilize against powerful private interests. This, then, is what the idea of 'state–society synergy' means: 'It is shorthand for the myriad concrete relationships of mutual support that connect communities, NGOs and social movements with individuals and organizations inside the state who put a priority on livelihood and sustainability', though this should not be taken to imply that conflict is absent from the relations of communities and state agencies. Quite to the contrary, paradoxically, 'conflict is likely to be first and foremost with agencies that are supposed to be part of the solution'. A political process is necessarily involved.[22]

Conclusion

I said at the beginning of this chapter that I thought that 'the Evans group' is actually much more critical of Putnam's conception of social capital than its members seem to be ready to state. Their work convincingly shows that the implications of the primary social ties and local social networks that have been elevated into the 'missing link' in development depend upon the wider socio-political context. Their work also shows up the very positive results that can follow from the establishment of what they label as 'synergy' across the public–private divide, between state agencies and communities or groups of people as citizens. But these results are not simply achieved by administrative fiat (such as the introduction of decentralized government institutions, or perhaps the funding of horizontal/local associations) for they involve a political process which is itself greatly influenced by the nature of underlying social conflicts and the nature and extent of inequality. As we will see in the next chapter, these implicitly radical ideas have been sought to be neutralized, rather systematically, in the official discourse of social capital.

6

The Trojan Horse?

Social Capital in the World Bank

The thoughts and actions of 'development' bureaucrats are powerfully shaped by the world of acceptable statements and utterances within which they live; and what they do and do not do is a product not only of the interests of various nations, classes or international agencies, but also of a working out of this complex structure of knowledge.

James Ferguson[1]

Despite their force, the critiques of Putnam's history and logic have proven ineffectual. In spite of (or because of?) the lack of an adequate theory of trust or of social capital within his work (a lack which is established in chapter 3 above), it has been remarkably seductive, and efforts are being made to apply it very widely. A number of writers comment upon the lack of clarity surrounding the whole concept of social capital but then proceed cheerfully to use it nonetheless as a metaphor, or as an 'heuristic device', and even sometimes – in spite of their reservations as to what it really means – as an 'analytical tool'. With hindsight it can be seen that around 1995 there was a 'big bang' and that since then the idea of social capital has expanded outwards across the range of the social sciences and through many different public sector bureaucracies.[2] There are by now several hundred references in the 'Library' which can be accessed from the World Bank's Social Capital website; others from the website of the Social Capital Interest Group at the University of Michigan – though some of the papers listed there represent retrospective claims that writers of the stature of E P Thompson *really* were talking about social capital when they thought they were writing about something else. Social capital is held to have the potential to make an immense contribution to social and economic development (which is the claim that I am most concerned with in this book); to solve the problems of health services; to improve performance in and of schools; to tackle family problems; to regenerate communities; to create more efficient commercial organizations; to build democracy and make collective action possible. None of this should surprise us, following Robert Putnam's apparent demonstration of the correlation between the incidence of social capital in America and the health, wealth and wisdom of Americans. But still, the fact that the idea of social capital took off in quite the way it has done surely cannot be explained entirely by the blandishments of Putnam's prose and the neatness of his statistics. He has clearly found a receptive audience, influenced variously by new currents of thought in economics and by communitarian philosophies, as well as by the pressures working within and upon the World Bank – which, both as the most important development research organization[3] and as a critically influential international financial institution, is most responsible for the explosion of social capital.

'Getting the social relations right': development thinking at the millennium[4]

The little phrase 'getting the social relations right' is a favourite of Michael Woolcock's, a clever sociologist who is one of the leading thinkers on social capital in the World Bank.[5] It is a sharp insight into the present state of development thinking, and shows why the idea of social capital has been found so powerful.

    The state-led approach to social and economic development – influenced by Keynesian economics, and put into effect through planning – was almost unquestioned until well into the 1970s, and was exemplified in many ways in the programmes of the World Bank.[6] It was called into question, and then swept aside, in the 1980s. In 1983, for example, Deepak Lal published an influential tract entitled *The Poverty of 'Development Economics'*,[7] in which he argued that the state is essentially predatory, and should therefore be 'rolled back'. Meanwhile ideas like Lal's were being given concrete expression in the development policies that were then being enjoined upon many developing countries in the stabilization and structural adjustment programmes of the International Monetary Fund and the World Bank. As it has been put, 'modernization' gave way to neo-liberalism, in what came to be known as 'the Washington consensus' (the 'consensus' referred to being that among development agencies, particularly the IMF and the Bank, located in Washington DC).[8] The starting point for ideas that came to command general agreement was with the view that markets should be left to themselves, and that economic development would then more or less take care of itself – and after that other problems which had been sought to be addressed, like poverty, would too. In short, it meant that 'the means [of development] – market forces – became an end in themselves'.[9] What passed for 'development thinking' became focused upon the issue of 'state vs market', with the outcome foretold. Important elements in the new consensus were: fiscal discipline and the reorientation of public expenditure (supposedly) towards carefully targeted social expenditure; tax reform (which in practice often meant less progressive taxation); trade and financial liberalization; the elimination of barriers to Foreign Direct Investment; and the building of a competitive market economy by privatizing and deregulating (including the labour market), and by ensuring secure property rights.

By the 1990s, however, some aspects, at least, of the Washington consensus had been criticized (though unnoticed, it seems, by the architects of India's economic reforms, initiated in 1991) – both from without and even from within the international financial institutions themselves. It was not just that critics associated with the United Nations Development Programme called for 'adjustment with a human face' – taking greater account of welfare needs in the process of adjustment – but also that assessments made by the IMF and Bank themselves showed that the new policies did not always appear to be as successful as had been expected.[10] Several currents of thought came together in such a way as to start to 'bring the state back in'. Research on the highly successful 'tiger economies' of East Asia began to show that their achievements seemed to depend not on 'free markets', but rather upon 'governing the market', involving an active industrial policy pursued by the state.[11] Thus it was argued that the most successful late developing economies had 'developmental states', headed by powerful (and generally repressive) elites, and with competent economic bureaucracies, insulated from politics, having the authority to direct and manage economic and social development in the pursuit of national economic interests. Meanwhile, a number of economic theorists who had for some time been pursuing work on 'institutions' – understood as the rules, norms and conventions that frame economic life and make it possible (given the imperfect knowledge and hence the risks that exist in the real world and limit exchange, even if not in the conventional model of the market in mainstream neo-classical economics) – were becoming more prominent.[12] Their thinking was reflected in the increasing attention which began to be placed upon 'governance', or sometimes 'good government', in the World Bank.[13] Simply put, it began to be recognized in development thinking that even the package of 'the Washington consensus' depends upon the existence of institutions established by states, and the bureaucratic organizations which implement them. It was not, and is not, the case that the argument about the centrality of the market has been conceded; rather, it has been recognized that 'making markets work (better)' depends upon government; and even that 'The state has an important role to play in appropriate regulation, industrial policy, social protection and welfare'.[14] Thus it is that some scholars and commentators have now started to speak of 'the post-Washington consensus' – one that rejects the analytical agenda of state vs market and argues instead that the two must complement each other. It is still a long way, however, from the old (broadly Keynesian) approach to economic development, and there is no sense in which the core ideas of the Washington consensus have been 'overturned'.

The point, for the purposes of the present discussion, is that current thinking about development is greatly concerned with 'good government', which is held to mean government that is transparent and accountable, working within a clear and consistent legal framework, such as will provide the conditions for effective and efficient markets. It is in this context that ideas about 'civil society', 'decentralization', 'participation' and latterly – in some senses, queen of them all, because it embraces them all – 'social capital', have acquired such currency. The basic idea is that through 'participation' in 'voluntary local associations' (which may be confused with 'non-governmental organizations') people are 'empowered' in 'civil society' (defined as the sphere of voluntary rather than ascriptive association, that lies outside the state and the family and kinship). A vibrant civil society, which implies the presence of a strong sense of civic and community responsibility among people, acts both as a vital check upon the activities and the agencies of the state, and as a kind of a conduit between the people and the government. A strong civil society should contain the expansion of the state (because people will oppose the invasion of 'their' space by the state), and will make for 'good government' (that is, 'democratic', meaning responsive, accountable and transparent government). It is expected, too, that in the context of such a strong civil society people will be broadly supportive of the market-led orientation of economic policy (which respects their rights to make 'choices'). Some statements of what constitutes 'good government' actually say that the pursuit of policies that are supportive of markets are as much a part of what it means as 'responsiveness', 'accountability' and 'transparency'. In these formulations of it, therefore, 'good government' actually transcends democracy. 'Decentralization' of government should facilitate all of this, partly because it is at local levels that citizens' or community action is most effective. The whole set of ideas is pitched specifically against the old 'top-down' development, which is seen as having failed. It is an extension to the old 'Washington consensus' rather than a radical rethinking of it ('post' Washington consensus, perhaps, but not 'past').

Given the currency of these ideas by the mid-1990s, it is not at all surprising that the idea of social capital, as it was expressed by Robert Putnam in *Making Democracy Work*, should have proven so attractive. Putnam seemed to have demonstrated that people participating in 'horizontal', voluntary associations, in civil society – what he called at first 'civic involvement' or 'civic engagement', and only later 'social capital' – was (measurably) good for government, and good for economic development. Although he himself had been rather pessimistic about the chances of escaping from the historical path dependence apparently exhibited by the institutional patterns of different societies, his work seemed to show that 'getting the social relations right' matters a great deal.

It also resonated with other ideas that were then becoming very fashionable across the political spectrum in both the United States and the United Kingdom – those of the 'new Communitarianism'. The sociologist Amitai Etzioni of the George Washington University, the principal spokesman of this movement, was feted by President Clinton and by political leaders in Britain, including Tony Blair.[15] The central tenets of Communitarianism are that there is a need for moral reconstruction in Western societies, drawing on the recognition that it is possible for there to be too strong an emphasis upon (individual) 'rights' and that 'strong rights presume strong responsibilities', thus steering a way between 'the anarchy of extreme individualism and the denial of the common good (and on the other hand) the collectivism that views itself as morally superior to its individual members'. Etzioni states the credo of the Communitarian movement, including the following clauses:

> We hold that the pursuit of self-interest can be balanced by a commitment to the community, without requiring us to lead a life of austerity, altruism or self-sacrifice . . .

> We hold that powerful special-interest groups . . . can be curbed without denying legitimate interests and the right to lobby . . .

> We hold these truths as Communitarians, as people committed to creating a new moral, social and public order based on restored communities, without allowing puritanism or oppression . . .

He goes on to say, 'If we are to have a more decent world, you and I must actively advance Communitarian ideas and ideals across neighbours' fences, in town hall meetings, in political debates . . . the country needs groups of people concerned with bolstering our families, schools, and neighbourhoods – our communities on the local and national levels – as the main conduits of a moral revival.'[16] The correspondences with Putnam's work are unmistakable; and in this climate of ideas in Washington DC it is easy to understand how attractive the concept of social capital has appeared.

The idea of 'getting the social relations right' also strengthened the case for involving social scientists other than economists much more extensively in development policy-making and practice. Here at last was a strong justification for their specialisms and their expertise: markets, it seemed, do not automatically give rise to the 'right' institutions to make them work effectively and efficiently.[17] The historic experiment taking place in Russia by the early to mid-1990s demonstrated this very clearly. The case was made for putting more effort into understanding the social, political and cultural conditions that influence markets, and the idea of social capital seemed to offer an interesting and important new way of going about achieving that understanding. It was attractive too, no doubt, because the very language of 'social capital' seemed to bring these matters into the purview of economics, while parts of Putnam's argument, and even more strongly so Coleman's theorization of social capital as it had been popularized by Putnam's book, resonated with institutional and with information-theoretic economists. The foundation of Coleman's theory of social capital (and of his social theory as a whole) in the rational choice framework recommended it to economists in general, and it provided a further justification for the imperialist enterprise of contemporary economics in relation to the other social sciences. Are not other social phenonema than those which are narrowly 'economic' susceptible to analysis with the same conceptual tools? And don't those tools make for a more rigorous, more 'scientific' kind of knowledge than is derived (say) from the anthropologists' case studies? So the attractiveness of the idea of social capital was doubly assured: it brought in the 'social' (or the 'non-economic') from the cold, while still assuring the hegemony of economics.

But for some, like Woolcock and Anthony Bebbington in particular, it seemed to offer something else: nothing less than a way of changing the agenda as defined by the economics discipline. According to Michael Edwards, who as Senior Civil Society Specialist in the Bank worked with them, they believed that the recognition of the significance of 'getting the social relations right' created an opening.[18] The idea of social capital, they think, is a kind of 'Trojan horse' even in the citadel of the economists. Woolcock more or less said as much in a statement that he once made on the Bank's email discussion site on social capital:

> Several critics, not without justification, have voiced their
> concern that collapsing an entire discipline into a single
> variable (especially one with such economic overtones) is a
> travesty, but there are others who are pleased that main-
> stream sociological ideas are finally being given their due at
> the highest levels. For them the term 'social capital' is as
> much good marketing as it is pragmatic theory! I tend to
> side with those in the latter camp . . .[19]

I believe that this view is sadly mistaken and that social capital has
rather led to the domestication – through the kind of dumbing
down that has gone on – of critical social science. In what follows
I aim to show this in an examination of the World Bank's Social
Capital website, and then in chapter 7, through a more detailed
consideration of several studies (including Bebbington's valuable
work on rural development in the Andes) that have aimed to use
the idea of social capital as an analytical tool.

The 'missing link' uncovered

A critical reading of the World Bank's construction of social capital

The idea of social capital was really not an established part of the
'development' lexicon until about 1997. Now it is the subject of
an attractive and well-produced website (accessible at:
www.worldbank.org/poverty/scapital) that is a mine of information, and deserves careful critical reading. The Home Page
carries the headline: 'Increasing evidence shows that social cohesion – social capital – is critical for poverty alleviation and
sustainable human and economic development', which strikes
one immediately as a rather conservative statement ('Social order
is good for you'). It also reflects the view of 'social capital'
advanced by Putnam and seems to take no account of the ideas of
'the Evans group' (discussed in chapter 5). A prominently dis-
played box defines social capital as 'the norms and social relations
embedded in the social structures of societies that enable people
to coordinate action to achieve desired goals'. The Home Page
connects the reader to a series of articles about social capital –
'What is social capital?', 'How is social capital measured?', 'Why

is it relevant to development?' – and on 'Social capital and World Bank projects'. It connects also to a series of descriptions of 'Sources of SC' and of 'Topics in SC'; to a Library which offers a number of Key Readings that can be downloaded, as well as a database of abstracts of articles about social capital; and to an email discussion group and various other 'resources'.

The first definition the reader is offered of social capital is not a great start, it has to be said. A charitable view of it is that it is tautological. Surely it is part of the definition of 'society' that it involves social relationships, which give rise to and are founded upon norms? And all societies involve some coordination of action between people (isn't this what norms are about?). So the first shot at definition on the website quite fails to give any clear or precise idea of what social capital is about, and it would seem that it is something that all societies must have. So what is it that can possibly make this mysterious substance so special and important as to be described as the 'missing link'?

The statement on 'What is social capital?', reached from the Home Page, is more helpful. Here the reader is told that 'Social capital refers to the institutions, relationships and norms that shape the quality and quantity of a society's social interactions', which is at least suggesting that 'it', whatever it is, produces variations (in terms of 'quality' and 'quantity') between societies. But then the impression of mistiness comes in again when the statement goes on 'Social capital is not just the sum of the institutions which underpin a society – it is the glue which holds them together'. What is this 'glue', then? The remainder of the statement goes some way to making this clear. We are told, at last, that, 'A narrow view of social capital regards it as a set of horizontal associations between people, consisting of social networks and associated norms that have an effect on community productivity and well-being. Social networks can increase productivity by reducing the costs of doing business ['It's not what you know, but who you know' again]. Social capital facilitates coordination and cooperation.' Or, in other words, contacts between people through social networks of one sort or another can make doing business, or politics easier. This is why, for example, the rich peasants in the village where I once lived in Tamil Nadu in south India have built up kinship networks extending over a wide geographical area and connecting city and country, that can sensibly be understood in terms of economic and political strategies. Something more tangible emerges here from the mists of the earlier statements we have been offered: social networks and norms of behaviour associated with them (though it appears that social networks may both give rise to social capital and actually *are* social capital, which is a bit confusing).

'Downsides' and 'bonding' and 'bridging'

A 'broader understanding of social capital', however – the statement continues – includes 'vertical as well as horizontal associations between people, and includes behaviour within and among organizations, such as firms'. The clarity of the sentences about social networks begins to recede. For one thing, it seems that is not just 'networks', but also 'behaviour within organizations' (not quite the same thing as networks) that can either constitute or give rise to social capital. There is an unstated reference here to a whole body of thought in economics and management which has to do with the role of 'trust' in organizations. But the implication is not pursued.

The main point that is being made here appears in the next sentence:

> This view recognizes that horizontal ties are needed to give communities a sense of identity and common purpose, but it also stresses that without 'bridging' ties that transcend various social divides (e.g. religion, ethnicity, socio-economic status), horizontal ties can become a basis for the pursuit of narrow interests, and can actively preclude access to information and material resources that would otherwise be of great assistance to the community (e.g. tips about job vacancies, access to credit).

The point that 'social capital' resides in both vertical and horizontal associations is perhaps an obvious one (just as it is clear to me that having good connections with, say, those I work with who are also migrants from my home town is an asset to me, so it is clear that it is an asset if I have some contacts with outsiders – local businessmen, perhaps, or officials – in powerful positions, who may be able and willing to help me), but it is extremely important for the Bank's arguments. For it is part of the response to the immediate objection (to the claim that social capital is 'good for development') that special interest groups of various kinds, like cartels and mafias, which do not stand for the wider social interest, are also strong social networks characterized by or embodying social capital;[20] and to the objection that 'strong social capital' within a particular social group may well depend upon exclusion of others, for example those from another caste group. As one of the Bank's social capital theorists, Deepa Narayan puts it, 'Social capital can explain much social exclusion, because the same ties that bind also exclude.'[21] The Bank is anxious to recognize that social capital also has a 'downside', in the formulation of Alejandro Portes,[22] who is one of the few critics of the notion of social capital to find a home on the website; and the statement says explicitly that 'communities, groups or networks which are isolated, parochial, or working at cross-purposes to society's collective interests (e.g. drug cartels, corruption rackets) can actually hinder economic and social development'. So not all social capital (= social networks) is of a socially positive kind, as I explained in chapter 1. Implicitly or explicitly, this warning – which is repeated at different points across the website – is there to ensure that, taking account of the 'downside', or 'dark side' of social capital,[23] 'developers' will be able to realise the 'upsides'. So social capital is saved for the angels. But there is a need, too, both for what has come to be called 'bonding capital' ('ties that give communities a sense of identity and common purpose') and 'bridging capital' (the 'ties that transcend various social divides'). These ideas have some resonance, perhaps, with those of the 'Evans group', but they specifically exclude any reference to the state or to relations across the public–private divide.

Most recently Woolcock and some of his colleagues in the Bank have proposed the three-fold distinction referred to in chapter 1 of this book, between:

> *bonding social capital*: strong ties between immediate family members, neighbours, close friends, and business associates sharing similar demographic characteristics;

bridging social capital: weaker ties between people from different ethnic, geographical and occupational backgrounds but with similar economic status and political influence;

linking social capital: ties between poor people and those in positions of influence in formal organizations such as banks, agricultural extension offices, schools, housing authorities, or the police.[24]

The new category of 'linking capital' implicitly, at least, acknowledges the ideas about 'synergy' from Peter Evans and his colleagues, albeit completely stripped of the emphasis that they place upon the socio-political context. Woolcock and his associates argue that 'A three-pronged approach by NGOs, firms and government agencies is essential to mobilize bonding social capital within communities; build more extensive bridging social capital to markets; and to enhance linking social capital to public institutions'. It is striking that there is no mention of 'political parties' here, and my discussion in chapter 1 raises questions about the (depoliticizing) politics of these proposals, particularly that concerning 'linking capital' – because it implies acceptance and even reinforcement of existing power structures. There is no hint of a recognition of what Evans concluded about the importance of the underlying social relations and the extent and nature of inequality. These problems are highlighted in a review by Jo Beall of research on social networks and organizations in nine cities of Africa, Asia and Latin America (including Bangalore, Ahmedabad and Vizakhaptnam, in India). Beall writes:

it is important not to over-romanticize the role of community organizations [which have a 'linking' role] . . . They too are underpinned by the fragility of members and actors, often bound together in vertical social relationships, as evidenced by the report on Colombo (Sri Lanka) . . . While the Community Development Councils [established there by government as part of its urban development programme] are designed to make government policy more participatory and equitable they are located, nevertheless, within established power structures and social relations. These in turn generate vertical patron–client relations. [And] both in the

Kumasi (Ghana) and Mombasa (Kenya) studies evidence is presented to show how traditional structures and ethnic politics serve to gate-keep opportunity, promote nepotism and corruption and foster insecurity. Clearly the social resources of the poor are frequently embedded in asymmetrical social relationships and engagement with government simply means reinforcing or exacerbating existing hierarchies or inequalities.[25]

A wider understanding of social capital...

Returning to the website statement on 'What is social capital?', we find that it concludes as follows:

> The broadest and most encompassing view of social capital includes the social and political environment that shapes social structure [at last!] and enables norms to develop. This analysis extends the importance of social capital to the most formalized institutional relationships and structures, such as government, the political regime, the rule of law, the court system, and civil and political liberties. This view not only accounts for the virtues and vices of social capital, and the importance of forging ties within and across communities, but recognizes that the capacity of various social groups to act in their interest depends crucially on the support (or lack thereof) that they receive from the state as well as the private sector. Similarly, the state depends on social stability and widespread popular support. In short, economic and social development thrives when the representatives of the state, the corporate sector, and civil society create forums in and through which they can identify and pursue common goals.

The reference here to the role of the state, and to state agencies, represents at least a nod in the direction of the 'Evans group' and of the critics of the World Bank usage of the idea of 'social capital' (or of Putnam's elevation of 'horizontal association' in civil society as the *primum mobile* of 'good government' and everything else, that I discussed in chapters 3 and 4). The statement also reflects 'the post-Washington consensus' on development policy, and the emphasis that came to be placed during the 1990s on 'good government' as a condition for successful economic development. But it also shows what a very big bag the idea of social capital has been woven into. This is both a strength and a weakness. It certainly helps to explain the great success of the idea, for 'social capital' takes account, it seems, of a wide range of social phenomena. But does it have any specific analytical content, at least without a lot of contextualizing commentary? This is a centrally important question to which I shall return. In practice the idea of social capital has, thus far, most commonly been translated into meaning 'membership in groups' or 'voluntary associations'.

... but then reduced again to 'local associations'

The paper that first elaborated the notion of social capital as the 'missing link' immediately refers to the problem that 'There is no consensus about which aspects of inter-action and organization merit the label of social capital' and it goes on to distinguish three usages.[26] One, which it associated with Putnam (see chapter 2 above), locates social capital in 'horizontal associations'; a broader conception, covering a wider range of types of associations, is associated with James Coleman (see above, in chapters 1 and 2); and, third, the even more encompassing view which effectively equates social capital with the entire institutional framework of a society is associated with the (liberal) institutional theorists Mancur Olson and Douglass North.[27] Yet, it is suggested, the three views have common features and it is concluded, with little discussion of the point, that 'the three definitions of social capital are not really alternative views, but rather complementary dimensions of the same process'. Under any of the definitions social capital is held to affect development outcomes through information-sharing (group-based lending schemes are mentioned in particular), coordination of activities (as by water- and forest-users' groups), and collective decision-making, all of which are themselves influenced by the 'macro-level social capital' in the institutional framework of the society as a whole.

The argument would only be a restatement of the simple

proposition that 'organization matters' were it not for the fact that the paper – reflecting the dominating influence of Putnam – consistently highlights the role of what it refers to as 'local associations'. It is recognized that such institutions may be most effective at enforcing cooperative action 'when the local distribution of assets is more equal'; that local institutions of this kind may be captured by those with local power; that 'The application of social capital in development is not a resource-neutral process'; and that by themselves – without other resources – these associations may not make much of a difference. All of which is very sensible. Yet the paper still concludes with strong recommendations about the role of donors and of governments in promoting 'desirable forms of social capital', which are in turn equated with 'local-level social capital' (some circularity of argument here), with local government, and with NGOs.

And by now, as Ben Fine has said,[28] studying the economic consequences of 'membership in groups' or 'local associations' has become almost a cottage industry. It has been the most influential way in which social capital has been sought to be measured.

Measuring social capital

The social capital website paper on 'How is social capital measured?' begins with the sentence: 'Social capital has been measured in a number of innovative ways, though for a number of reasons obtaining a single "true" measure is probably not possible, or perhaps even desirable.' This seems like an admission of the woolliness of the idea. Thus far, readers of the material on the website may surely be forgiven if they are still not entirely sure what is being talked about, or whether – in particular – social capital *is* 'social networks' or 'norms and values' (like those which are productive of trust, presumably), or whether it is rather the *effects* of norms and social networks. This is not at all an insignificant point. Do all those who participate in extensive social networks 'have social capital'? Or is it only those whose social networks actually deliver in terms of, say, jobs or credit? Again an observation from experience of village India is relevant. In the village in Tamil Nadu where I lived in the early 1970s it was readily apparent that being a member of the locally dominant caste mattered. A landless labourer who was an Agamudaiyan Mudaliar was invariably better off than a landless labourer from among the Dalits because of his social connections. But this didn't mean that the Dalits were not plugged into extensive social networks. Wherein lies, or what is the 'social capital' here?

In practice, as the website paper documents, some well-regarded studies have used indicators of trust and 'civic norms' from the World Values Survey, rather as proxies for the strength of 'civic associations'; and perhaps most influentially Narayan and Pritchett from the World Bank used data from a large-scale survey conducted in Tanzania to construct a measure of social capital, which they call the 'Putnam index'. Interestingly these two writers say, 'Social capital, while not all things to all people, is many things to many people.' They continue, 'A dramatic restriction of the scope of what one might mean by "social capital" must precede any attempt to measure it . . . Beginning from Putnam's analysis we define social capital as the density and nature of the network of contacts or connections amongst individuals in a given community (for instance whether groups are "horizontal" or "vertical" or "inclusive" or "exclusive" in membership) . . .'[29] In other words, they follow the approach that was taken by Cristiaan Grootaert in the 'missing link' paper, though for more explicit, pragmatic reasons. Their index was finally constructed from: four sub-indices on the number of groups of which an individual was a member; their kin heterogeneity; income heterogeneity; and group functioning. Famously, Narayan and Pritchett showed in the end that 'Higher village social capital is associated with higher levels of individual's incomes, even after controlling for household education, physical assets and village characteristics'. This work, following Putnam's, probably more than any other, launched the career of the idea of social capital, and it confirmed the focus in particular on membership in groups and especially in voluntary associations. Moreover, in their estimation, 'The quantitative effect of social capital is surprisingly large: a one standard deviation increase in village social capital predicts expenditures per person (our proxy for income) increase by 20 or 30 per cent for each household in the village. This impact is as large as *tripling* either the level of education or stock of non-farming assets.' This helps to account for the triumphant announcement of the discovery of the 'missing link' in development. In the light of evidence like this it is only the most embittered cynics, surely, who would want to respond, 'How very convenient (in these times of calls for public expenditure cuts). So there is not such a need for investment in education, after all. People just need to get together more!'

Still, Narayan and Pritchett's work is certainly important. A somewhat similar piece, though it does not supply such impressive statistics – also accessible from the website – is by Krishna and Uphoff on 'Mapping and Measuring Social Capital' with reference to watershed management in Rajasthan. They found that measures of social capital like that constructed by Putnam in his Italian study simply don't work in the Rajasthan context, where formally constituted associations hardly exist and newspaper readership is very low. So they constructed a measure of social capital by combining responses to interview questions relating to 'structural' forms of social capital (networks and roles) and to cognitive forms (norms, values, attitudes and beliefs). And they found that social capital, thus measured, 'is related positively and consistently with superior development outcomes both in watershed conservation and in cooperative development activities more generally'.[30] This does not really seem very surprising, and their study, even more than Narayan and Pritchett's, leaves the reader casting around for an understanding of the circumstances and the social processes that give rise to the observed results. Such exercises in statistical correlation are more intriguing than they are informative.

These quantitative exercises have, however, been extremely influential. 'Policy makers' have understandable difficulty in confronting the messiness of social reality, and they necessarily resort to frameworks that seem to cut through the complexity. Narayan and Pritchett's findings have powerfully legitimized the notion that 'local organization' is a key to successful development.[31] It is salutary, therefore, to read the results of ethnographic research. Beall's work, again, is helpful:

The balance of the evidence suggests that the social resources of the poor constitute more private than public goods as social networks exclude as much as they include. At the same time, if the benefits accrue to groups, then those who enjoy them may fare better than those who do not and as such it is perhaps safe to call them semi-public goods.

However, these in turn reflect and promote the correspon-
ding social structure, for the social resources of rich families
in Kumasi, networks of businessmen in Ahmedabad or
ethnic groupings in Mombasa clearly far exceeded those of
many groups of the urban poor, even when the latter were
far greater in number. There are class and educational differences in the measures of social resources on which people
can draw and the efficacy with which they can employ them
in relation to urban governance. Moreover, as observed elsewhere and in the city studies where family ties (have been)
shown to be key resources, the poor have weak bonds which,
while providing some semblance of security in times of
need, serve to exclude them from broader social processes.
Thus in terms of causal pathways, social capital understood
in terms of social resources is not necessarily a good predic-
tor of poverty reduction strategies or pro-poor urban
governance.[32]

'Local organization' has to be viewed in the context of the overall structure of social relations, and of power.

'Why is social capital relevant to development work?'

The Bank website text argues that 'Conventional prescriptions for
enhancing the economic prospects of communities and nations
include improving education and health facilities, constructing
competent and accountable political institutions, and facilitating
the emergence of free markets able to compete in the global economy' (do 'markets' compete, incidentally?). Social capital, it goes
on, 'speaks to each of these aspects'. For example: 'Schools [and
health care facilities, too] are more effective when parents and
local citizens are actively involved. Teachers are more committed,
students achieve higher test scores, and better use is made of school
facilities in those communities where parents and citizens take an
active interest in children's educational well-being.' This is a familiar observation in my own country (the United Kingdom). But it is
also the case that such active involvement is generally more characteristic of the wealthier, 'professional' or middle class parts of our
cities. The Russian case, the text continues, 'highlights how not
understanding pre-existing forms of social capital can hinder policy

implementation', referring to the way in which the strength of nepotism and of ethnic factions alongside the weakness of the rule of law has upset the privatization process there.

The next, and in some ways most extraordinary part of the text, then refers to 'Social capital and access to formal markets'. It reads: 'Securing access to markets is a crucial step along the path to economic advancement for the poor. One of the defining features of being poor is that one lacks connections into the formal economy including material and informational resources. The poor's social capital, derived primarily from family and neighbours, can serve as an important day-to-day "safety-net", but the social capital possessed by the rich enables them to further their interests. Helping the poor to transcend their closed networks in order to access additional resources is one of the challenges of economic development.' This shows little advance from the Sector Paper on Rural Development of 1975 (which equated the way out of poverty with 'the modernization and monetization of rural society and . . . its transition from traditional isolation to integration with the national economy'[33]). No more now than a quarter of a century ago have the World Bank specialists taken account of research like that of Krishna Bharadwaj,[34] showing that the poor don't necessarily 'lack connections' at all with 'the formal [i.e., presumably, monetary] economy', and rather that their poverty is reproduced precisely through the ways in which they are incorporated into markets. This statement from the website does at least recognize one aspect of the differentiation between 'rich' and 'poor', but the final sentence is a remarkably blithe piece of skating over the problems of economic power. We might be able to agree that 'helping the poor to transcend their closed networks in order to mobilize in support of demands for the redistribution of land, or for the payment of decent wages (and thus "access additional resources")' – for example – is indeed 'one of the challenges of development'. But this is probably not what the Bank's specialists had in mind.

Social capital has lots of implications for development projects. Findings about social capital reinforce the 'growing body of evidence that incorporating the poor into the design and implementation of development projects helps not only to produce more appropriate projects, but it ensures that they are better targeted to reach those with the greatest needs'. Consequently one of the principal policy prescriptions that has been derived in part from work on social capital is that 'participation' should play 'an increasingly important role in how the World Bank designs, implements and evaluates projects and policies'. It also confirms the Bank's interest in 'partnerships' between different 'development actors' – governments, civil society organizations, the private sector and aid agencies – not least because these both draw upon and help to build more 'bonding' and 'linking capital'.

Finally, then, the website papers highlight what needs to be done, or what can be done – by donors – in order to integrate concern for positive construction of and upon social capital in their work, drawing upon Grootaert's 'missing link':

identify existing pockets of social capital [given the elusiveness of most forms of social capital this perhaps really means 'associations' of one sort and another] and take care not to destroy them by disabling partnerships and breaking down social cohension [as through liberalization and structural adjustment programmes?];

use local-level social capital and participation to deliver projects. For example, a cooperative credit system may function more smoothly among women who already have relationships and a history of networking together to reach common goals [but what about women from the poorest social groups, say in Bangladesh, where it is known that they do not participate very much in the activities of the Grameen Bank?];

create an environment which enables social capital to thrive by providing infrastructure which helps people communicate better and promoting the rule of law which provides opportunities for recourse if partnerships or associations go awry;

invest in social capital directly and indirectly through participatory project design and implementation and fostering cross-sectoral partnerships for development;

promote social capital learning and research.

There is much here that seems on the face of it to be perfectly sensible. The problem lies in the context in which these ideas are projected, which systematically veils the nature of power and the ways in which it creates the conditions for mass poverty.

One last, particular point here, concerning the last of these injunctions – 'promote social research and learning'. The World Bank has set up a number of initiatives precisely to promote this research and learning, including the website itself and the many resources which can be accessed from it. But it is striking that the database in the 'Library' includes very little reference to work published outside the United States – and notably not to that which has been critical of the concept.[35] In part this may be a sad reflection of the relative weakness of the social sciences outside the USA, but it also reflects the hegemonizing nature of the social science on which the Bank's research effort is largely built – social science which is founded on methodological individualism and rational choice theorizing, and which is uncomfortable both with history and with the problem of power.[36]

Conclusion

Close examination of the material which is available on or accessed through the World Bank Social Capital website confirms the argument of this book as a whole: that elaboration of the idea of 'social capital' has mystified rather than clarified – but mystified to good effect from the viewpoint of the protagonists of economic liberalization and globalization. It is not clear whether we should consider social capital as being constituted by, or residing in, social networks, or whether social capital is rather to be thought of as the effects of these networks. Reflection on this problem relates to another, that of whether 'social capital' means anything at all apart from the context – notably the context of relationships of power (my problem with the networks of Dalits as opposed to those of Agamudaiyans in a Tamil village, for instance). On one level, we are told, social capital resides in the entire structure of the institutions of a society. But it can then be specified only in terms of the metaphor of 'glue'; and it seems that all societies must, by definition, have 'social capital' in this sticky sense. World Bank specialists themselves tell us that 'social capital means many things to many people', and then they actually end up by focusing on 'membership in groups' or 'voluntary associations'. Talking about social relationships as a form of 'capital' no doubt has the effect of bringing them within the compass of the dominant mode of thought within economics. It is also clear that part of the attraction of the idea, and why it has taken off in the way that it has, is precisely that it is a capacious bag allowing for different understandings and different interpretations. This often makes for successful ideas in the development discourse (that of 'sustainable development', invoked on the Social Capital website home page, is another case in point).

But I have also been able to show the ways in which the representation on the website of these often fuzzy ideas studiously ignores and so obscures problems that have to do with class and power. It is perhaps most significant that, in so far as the ideas of the 'Evans group' that I discussed in chapter 5 appear at all in these statements, they have been stripped of their strong emphasis on the socio-political context, including the extent of inequality in a society. There is not much evidence here that the idea of social capital is a 'Trojan Horse' capable of challenging the agenda of the World Bank's methodological individualist economists. Rather, it appears, as Ferguson found, that the 'social capitalists' have themselves been trapped within a particular social science discourse that ignores power. But we should look more closely at serious attempts to put the idea to work. This is the task of the next chapter.

7

Putting Social Capital to Work

What Happened to the Trojan Horse

The process of excising Bourdieu from social capital has had the effect of endowing social capital with an unlimited scope of application both in terms of what it is and in what effects it has.

Ben Fine[1]

It is not my purpose in this chapter to offer an exhaustive review of the social capital literature. Large numbers of papers have in any case recently been reviewed by Foley and Edwards, and by Ben Fine.[2] As Fine says, the manner of much of the work follows lines established earlier by James Coleman, and then by Putnam, and it has by now been replicated many times. A measure of social capital is established and it is then shown to be strongly correlated with an 'output' such as a measure of health. Not uncommonly the implication of these sorts of studies, as Virginia Morrow pointed out, is that social capital becomes 'part of what might be termed "deficit theory syndrome", yet another "thing" or "resource" that unsuccessful individuals, families, communities and neighbourhoods lack'.[3] In studies of this kind there may be – though there often is not – an attempt to explain, and less frequently an attempt to test, why the correlation indicates causality. Even careful studies that attempt to measure the effects of social capital are unsatisfactory because 'social capital' remains a statistical artefact, and the questions of what causes what, and by what mechanisms or social processes, remain unanswered. So here I want to look in some detail at several studies, in somewhat different fields, in which serious attempts have been made to use the concept of social capital analytically, and not just as a variable in correlation analysis. I have chosen research studies that are driven by practical policy concerns, but addressing different sorts of problems, and from different geographical contexts, in which social processes are examined directly, historically and ethnographically, rather than being inferred from statistical correlations. What the studies also have in common is that in all of them the researchers have sought, very honestly, to put the idea of social capital to work.

Reviews of these studies show, at least, that the idea of social capital doesn't add much. But beyond this, and much more significant, they show how its application detracts from recognition of power. The point is put very well, ironically enough by a World Bank author, in the course of a very worthy effort to realize the 'great potential' of social capital in the context of community development, when he says that 'social capital can also become an integral part of the structures of constraint created by gender, class, ethnicity, and in the case of India, religion and caste . . . (so) . . . we contend that the relevance of social capital cannot be fully assessed unless one considers the power relations that mediate social interaction'.[4] My reviews tend to confirm Fine's contention, cited at the head of this chapter – the balloon of social capital only flies once any baggage remaining from Bourdieu is thrown out. But this is to say, of course, that the concept of social capital that has expanded through the social sciences is the one that fails to confront issues of class relations and of power. Some 'Trojan Horse' for challenging the mainstream development agenda, or the hegemony of neo-classical economists.

'Bonding', 'bridging' and 'linking': rural development in the Andes

One of the most thorough-going and sustained efforts to use the idea of social capital analytically and to demonstrate its value has been that of a geographer, Anthony Bebbington, who has sometimes worked in the World Bank, and has done intensive research in different parts of the Andes, in South America.[5] His work starts with the observation that there are what he calls 'islands of sustainability' in the Andes, even though the general picture there may be one of concentrations of poverty, on fragile lands, and of consequent environmental degradation and out-migration. There are some areas in highland Bolivia and Ecuador 'where vicious cycles of poverty, degradation and out-migration, have been turned into virtuous circles in which growth, intensification [of land use and of livelihoods], resource restoration and organization seem to feed on each other'. These islands have features in common. They are associated with the production of high-value horticultural and dairy products for middle and high-income markets, but also with well-developed local organizations of indigenous farmers that are linked in regional and national networks, and which earlier helped to press for land reforms and contributed to the demise of former large highland estates. Crucially, in Bebbington's view, these organizations are also linked into wider networks, through the mediation of outsiders. In one case the key outsider was a university professor; in another it was a group of priests; in a third European volunteers. But 'In all the cases of success, outside intervention and key individuals have played critical roles . . . these individuals not only brought ideas, but more importantly they brought networks of contacts that helped bridge gaps between the locality and non-local institutions and resources'.[6]

These 'islands' of sustainable rural development in the Andes thus exemplify the general theoretical argument about social capital proposed by the sociologist Michael Woolcock who, as one of the leading figures in social capital research in the Bank, is a volunteer for – or perhaps the builder of – the Trojan Horse. The starting point of Woolcock's arguments, which I referred to in the last chapter, is with the recognition that social ties may involve costs as well as benefits. Group loyalties may involve extremely onerous obligations. This is reflected, for example, in the decisions of some members of immigrant communities in the USA to anglicize their names in order to avoid obligations to new arrivals from their original homes. Or, another instance: strong social ties may involve serious costs for people in terms of well-being foregone, if, as is the case in much of rural India, 'community expectations' mean that girls are kept out of school. It is clear, too, that some groups of people may have strong social ties among themselves, but still be lacking in influence or access to formal institutions. The most familiar dimensions of social capital are those Granovetter referred to as 'strong' and 'weak' ties, the former representing immediate family members, close friends, and professional colleagues, the latter encompassing more distant associates and acquaintances.[7] In the recent literature it has become popular to refer to these two dimensions as 'bonding' and 'bridging' social capital. The point is that – as Bebbington's analysis in the Andes so clearly shows – a successful development dynamic generally involves both 'bonding' and 'bridging' relationships. In the Andean 'islands' indigenous, local organizations have clearly played an important role, but success has also depended upon the existence of external networks. The one would not have worked, or worked very well, without the other. Bebbington speaks of 'the critical role of networks and organizations in bridging state, market and civic spheres, and in renegotiating the relationships among these spheres'. 'Bonding capital' – close ties among a group of people – on its own may be of value to them, but its costs (as with the immigrants to the USA whom I mentioned) may well outweigh the benefits, or on its own (as among the 'indigenous' communities of the Andes) it may not amount to much in terms of resources or opportunities. Or it may be that if there are strong ties within particular ethnic groups, for example among 'Muslims' and 'Hindus' in some Indian cities, in the absence of cross-cutting links or 'bridges' between them, there is a strong likelihood of conflict.[8] Equally, 'bridging capital' on its own may be of relatively little value to people if they lack a secure base.[9]

Latterly, Woolcock has distinguished the third, vertical dimension or form of social capital ('linking capital'), the significance of which is shown up in research that demonstrates how 'poverty is a function of powerlessness and exclusion, and that a key task for development practitioners is ensuring that the activities of the poor not only "reach out", but are also "scaled up". An important component of this strategy entails forging alliances with sympathetic individuals in positions of power, an approach Hirschman wryly calls "revolution by stealth"'.[10] Thus we have the threefold distinction developed by Woolcock and his co-workers, that appears in the *World Development Report 2000/2001* of the World Bank, and is discussed here in chapter 6. In these proposals existing power structures are taken as given. The possibility that through political organization and mass mobilization poorer people might actually struggle against 'exclusion' and 'lack of resources' (not just depend upon 'sympathetic individuals in positions of power'), and so bring about change in the distribution of power and resources does not even enter into consideration. It seems from Bebbington's account that the outsiders who were involved in all the successful cases that he studied have supplied 'linking capital'. Yet it is clear that not all such linkages can be construed in this positive manner. There are also linkages between subordinated people and those in positions of power which have the character of clientship and, far from making for 'revolution by stealth', are instrumental in securing the dominance of the power-holders.

An important part of Bebbington's argument is actually missing from the discussion of 'bonding', 'bridging' and 'linking' – a discussion that seems to offer such neat and logical solutions to the problems of development. Bebbington refers to the role of local, regional and national movements of indigenous farmers in pressing the case for land reforms. He says:

> Indigenous organizations have clearly played an important role in influencing trajectories of environmental and socio-economic change in the Andes. *They have done so in part by challenging, negotiating and influencing dominant institutions that marginalize the rural poor* . . . Initially these were challenges to the hacienda, the church and the state. *These were challenges that invoked claims for rights for the rural poor . . .'* (emphasis added).[11]

There is no explicit reference to such political struggles in Woolcock's abstractions about bonding, bridging and linking capital, and though they appear in Bebbington's later elaborations of his own arguments, they are referred to with the nicely neutral, technical language of 'access to resources'.[12] But Bebbington's most recent essay, drawing on these Andean materials, on 'Capitals and Capabilities: A Framework for Analyzing Peasant Viability, Rural Livelihoods and Poverty' finally sees him returning to the politics of class struggle – that are so obscured in the language of bonding, bridging and linking – when he argues:

> That state agencies and actors will respond in . . . constructive ways, or that efforts at popular organization will not meet with repression, violence or exclusion rather than

increased government responsiveness, is, of course, far from certain: indeed, it is often far from being even likely. This is important, for Putnam's – and other – discussions of social capital [Woolcock's for instance] often understate the 'rawer' questions of political economy and violence. Indeed, one of the most critical 'resources' that people need to access is the legalization and continuing recognition by government, military and society of rights of organization and association. Without these, struggles for access are quite likely to be unsuccessful and, indeed, repressed.[13]

In the end we wonder what, if anything, the idea of 'social capital' – whether broken down into its three variants or not – adds to Bebbington's generally persuasive analysis. It is not at all evident that the idea has an analytical content which advances the argument in any way, and the main effects of the language of social capital in World Bank-speak are to suggest that 'getting the social relations right' is a technical and not a political process. The language of social capital does indeed understate the tougher questions of political economy.

I will turn now to a piece of work in a very different context, and with more modest ambitions, but which also shows up the shallowness of a concept of social capital lightened by the jettisoning of the Bourdieuvian baggage of class.

Looking for social capital in East London

The Joseph Rowntree Foundation (established by the north of England business family of which Seebohm Rowntree, pioneer of scientific poverty research, was a member) supports social policy research in the United Kingdom, and 'since 1992 the JRF has been trying to discover what works in the regeneration of deprived neighbourhoods'.[14] This is what is attempted in a report entitled *Neighbourhood Images in East London: social capital and social networks on two East London Estates*.[15] The wider background to the study, the authors say, is in the 'strong governmental interest in communities and neighbourhoods', seen as they now are 'as central ingredients in the "Third Way" [which is supposed to blend the best features of planned and of market economies within a broadly liberal-democratic political framework], with its emphasis on partnership and cooperative self-help'.[16] They note that the approach has been influenced to some extent by 'communitarianism', the philosophy which advocates the promotion of a sense of social responsibility (as against 'rights'), based on restored communities and strengthened social networks. In the context of these sorts of ideas, clearly, the 'regeneration' of deprived neighbourhoods is something of particular concern. Given that 'deprivation' is at least partially equated with the notion of 'exclusion', or 'inadequate' social participation, and that the practical task is seen as being to increase 'social cohesion', it is easy to understand why the JRF researchers should have been attracted to the use of the idea of social capital as an 'analytical tool'. In defining social capital they say that it refers to 'our relations with one another, [encompassing] both formal and informal networks', which they imply corresponds with Putnam's idea of it.

In *Neighbourhood Images* the researchers aimed, through semi-structured interviews, focus group discussions and some participant observation in the estates they studied, to 'identify what aids social cohesion and contributes to the neighbourhood store of social capital'. Clearly, the ways in which people think about their neighbourhoods is a major influence on 'social cohesion', for only if people believe that others in their neighbourhood will generally reciprocate can it be said that something like a 'cohesive community' exists; and the idea of such a 'community' (or in other words a history of people supporting each other to an appreciable extent, and of enduring organization) is one of the few ways in which the idea of a 'stock' of social capital makes sense (to me, at any rate). So the research is about the perceptions and attitudes of people on the two East London estates towards their neighbourhoods, both as they think they actually are, and as they would like them to be; and about coping strategies and the role of neighbourhood networks in these; and the ways in which all of these things are influenced by housing design, facilities, and by regeneration initiatives.

The results show that 'neighbourhood images', as one might expect, change over time and vary significantly, both spatially – for example between people in different types of housing – and socially, as between elderly, middle-aged and young people. The researchers note that 'perceptions of division coexist with perceptions of cohesion', and they paint a picture of social contexts in which there is, arguably, a good deal of social capital, as they define it, but in which it is fragmented. Neighbourhood ties are very important to people, but the definition of the 'neighbourhood' varies between different people, and there is 'an evident tension between the desire on the part of some residents to mix with those similar to themselves, and the perceived need on the part of others to broaden individuals' social networks for wider social cohesion'.

So, what is to be done? In such circumstances how can 'social cohesion' be fostered? 'Policies and interventions which might help include: policies, amenities and organizations which foster the development of supportive networks and at the same time do not exclude newcomers from established patterns. Housing design and allocation are crucial, but so, too, is a plentiful mix of meeting places [different sorts of spaces where different groups of people can socialize] (etc.).' But there is also a requirement for 'a more equitable distribution of resources. Social cohesion is not advanced by their inegalitarian distribution . . . *The current "Third Way" policy emphasis on self-help for individuals and communities will be a slow starter in areas like the Keir Hardie estate unless facilities and resources are put back in*' (emphasis added; note the close connection here with the argument put in chapter 4 about the relationships between inequality and 'community' or social capital in the United States).[17] The fact is that resources matter for, even though they certainly do not of themselves create functioning communities, 'Resources impact on residential continuity, on interaction and socializing with fellow residents and workers; they can help to facilitate identity with and pride in the area, and can have a direct influence on some forms of anti-social behaviour'.

While they do not develop the point, in the end Cattell and Evans, the authors of *Neighbourhood Images*, express a sense of dissatisfaction or frustration with the brave idea of social capital with which they started. They conclude simply with the words, 'The evidence emphasizes that the concept of social capital is insubstantial without a material base.'[18] So much for the 'missing link' – which absolves the state of responsibilities and so means that it can be 'rolled back' – in this context. It is hard to avoid the conclusion that Cattell and Evans have foisted the idea of social capital upon themselves, driven to it by the bandwagon that has gathered so much momentum as a result of Putnam's brilliant proselytizing. But they have discovered for themselves what some of the theoretical critics of the idea of social capital have already pointed out: the conclusion that 'social capital' is entirely context-specific, and that the resources to which the idea refers are thoroughly implicated in relationships of power. Had they thought about social capital in the light of Bourdieu's conceptu-alization of it then they would not have started out with the expectations that they did.

My third example of an attempt at putting the idea of social capital to work reaches much more explicit conclusions about its limitations. Ironically, in view of the claims that are still made from within the Bank about social capital, most of which are sunk by this study, it is a World Bank paper.

Looking for social capital in the coalfields of Orissa

The study, *Exploring the Concept of Social Capital and its Relevance for Community-based Development, The Case of Coal-mining Areas in Orissa, India*, is by Enrique Pantoja of the South Asian Infrastructure Unit of the World Bank.[19] It seems, therefore, that the author was associated with the Bank's 'Coal Sector Rehabilitation Project', and that he is not in the first place a 'social capitalist'. The fact that he devotes part of his paper to quite a thorough-going critical review of the literature, referring to some sources (notably Bourdieu) which do not usually feature in Bank papers, seems to confirm that his really was an 'explo-ration' of the concept, and that he had not been trained to miss the (fairly) obvious problems with it. Right at the outset he pays due respect to Bank social capitalizing when he says that 'The potential contribution of social capital, or in simple terms civic engagement and social connectedness to development appears to be immense', but then he goes on almost immediately to note that 'The celebratory tone surrounding the notion of social cap-ital must be dealt with cautiously, and the concept investigated rigorously, however' – not least because there is still so much confusion about what the term actually *means*! The significance of social capital, he notes, is supposed to be that it facilitates access to other resources such as basic services, which are in turn instrumental in bringing about poverty-alleviation. This is the main reason for attempting to support and promote it, and why it is held to be such 'an important new dimension in community development' (exactly the idea which motivated the East London researchers, too). But what about access to social capital resources themselves? Pantoja starts to wonder, suggesting that 'under scarcity conditions . . . it (may) also become an integral part of the structures of constraint created by gender, class, ethnicity' (the statement I cited earlier). The relevance of social capital, then 'cannot be fully assessed unless one considers the power relations that mediate social interaction'.[20] The neophyte social capitalist – as I take Pantoja to be – seems to have got to the nub of the matter right at the outset.

The study is based on research in a number of villages in two somewhat contrasting coal-mining areas in Orissa, affected by the Coal Sector Rehabilitation Project. This project has two sets of objectives, reflected in its different components. One has to do with increasing the profitability of opencast mines, and the other with increasing the capacity of Coal India Ltd (CIL) to deal with the environmental and social issues which surround opencast mining – the latter having to do in particular with the needs for resettlement and rehabilitation of those affected by the mines. Pantoja was not evaluating the measures that are being taken under the World Bank-funded projects, but rather considering them as factors in the situation that he analysed, and in which he was trying 'to understand how social capital is created, destroyed and recreated along [*sic*: perhaps, 'along with'] processes of community-based development . . .' A fundamental factor in this case is that Coal India Limited has to a significant extent come to stand in the place of the state. It is a bureaucratic, profit-orientated organization, placed in the contradictory position of securing the conditions for profit-taking and of being made responsible for the welfare of people in the regions affected by its activities. Its 'capacity to address all the demands of the surrounding communities, let alone to fulfil its promises regarding resettlement and rehabilitation, is limited';[21] and the company is at once expected by people in the coal-mining areas to provide for them, and mistrusted.

Many of Pantoja's observations are familiar, from earlier village ethnographies. There is a lot of 'social capital' about in the Orissa villages he studied, in the sense that there are strong horizontal networks amongst people – but they are fragmented on caste lines:

> mutual trust exists in abundance, but it is highly fragmented, as a mechanism of inclusion/exclusion [essentially those principles on which the differentiation of castes rests] tends to operate very strongly among residents of the study areas to create closed groups . . . there might actually be an oversupply of certain forms of social capital [while there are no] large, continuous and interlocking networks of support.

The interventions of CIL have tended to accentuate divisions among people in local communities, because offers of employment in the mines, where wages are high, have been linked with land ownership. CIL has necessarily taken over a lot of land, and it has compensated landowners with jobs. Those who have not secured work in the company come particularly from lower castes and their livelihoods may well have tended to depend upon entering into patron–client relations with those who have. Further, 'in addition to a possible high level of identification with work, which would increase community cleavages even within similar caste or tribal groups, identity categories granted by Mahanadi Coalfields to allocate compensation packages for resettlement and rehabilitation might also contribute to fragment the social fabric even further'.[22]

Unsurprisingly in these circumstances in which residential 'communities' are cross-cut by such differences of identity and of power, what associational life there is (outside gender, caste and such class-based groups as there are) reflects the existing social structure: 'the decision-making process is usually dominated by the most powerful members, with the exception perhaps of the youth clubs'. The community development programmes that CIL is now undertaking involve the establishment of 'village working groups' which are supposed to ensure participation and build a sense of ownership of the assets which are provided amongst beneficiaries. 'These working groups are intended to have a village-wide membership, representative of all castes and tribal population, and to be concerned with the development needs of all the habitations within the boundaries of the (project) villages . . . The village working groups, however, have tended to reproduce the existing social structure and power relations.' Pantoja points out that any attempt at 'building' social capital in a context like that of the coal-mining villages of Orissa has to contend with the problem of establishing cooperation among very unequal partners; and also that the formation of social capital involving articulations between groups – in a union, for example – or across villages, may well be opposed by CIL because of its potential for triggering collective action liable to interfere with the company's interests.

He argues finally – like some of those who studied the community development programmes of the 1950s – that:

> the standard approach to community development has been based, at least in the Indian context, on unrealistic notions of the nature of community in the villages and of the possibilities and democratic content of collective action . . . there are three critical issues missing from these assumptions: (a) social capital is not inherently beneficial to all members of the community; (b) horizontal forms of social capital are important, but without vertical articulations the impact of community development efforts will be very constrained; and (c) external agents can help in facilitating the creation of social capital, but their presence can create dependency . . . [and] . . . sustainability of [such] induced social capital may be low.

The standard approach has been lacking because it has been assumed that communities are inherently democratic. They are not; *and without 'interventions to democratize community life'* (emphasis added) – though what these interventions might be is not explained – 'village-wide groups are not effective mechanisms for democratic planning and decision-making'.[23] This conclusion might have been anticipated, of course, from a reading of the work on social capital by the 'Evans group'.[24]

Pantoja's 'general discussion' in the conclusion of his report is so strikingly at odds with so much that is claimed about social capital by the World Bank (as on the Social Capital website), that I shall quote from it at length. He advances several key propositions on the basis of his research in Orissa mining villages, which correspond closely with the critique developed in chapters 2 to 5 in this book:

1. The basic points are these: *'Our analysis seems to indicate (that) it would be limiting to approach social capital by focusing exclusively on associational membership and norms of reciprocity and trust and by assuming that social capital always produces beneficial forms of civic engagement or that more of it is always better'*; and *'civic society and its social capital matter for community development, but in the context of government institutions and the general institutional framework of society at large'*. [Both these points were made, of course, by Peter Evans: see chapter 5 above].

2. 'Access to social capital is differential while its use value is context dependent. Accordingly the value-added of social capital resources to community development can be positive or negative.'

3. 'The value of a given form of social capital for enabling some action depends on the social and economic location of the social capital in a community.'

4. 'Although social relations are often a necessary condition for trust and trustworthy behaviour, they are not sufficient to ensure these [because of the 'dark side' of social capital which I have discussed in the preceding chapters].'

5. 'While certain studies (e.g. Putnam 1993) may have indicated that "civic engagement" leads to good governance, it is as likely that the causality may also work in the opposite direction, as historical evidence seems to indicate.' Further,

6. 'The networks and relationships created by association do not guarantee by themselves political outcomes . . . differential mobilization of the population can lead to the emergence of very particularistic demands (and, simply put, one person's civic society group can be another person's pressure group) . . . while the capacity of well-mobilized groups to make effective demands on government can remain limited.'

Finally the three key points are reiterated: (i) horizontal organization in civil society [*pace* the enthusiasts of the 'missing link'] cannot be assumed always to be in the interests of society at large; (ii) differentiation between different types of organizations must be made (football clubs and choirs are not the same as labour unions in terms of their implications and effects); and (iii) power relations should enter the evaluation of social capital . . . *Social capital matters, but its promotion should be framed within a process of democratization that should be an integral objective of community development.*[25]

This last point (which I have emphasized) really seems quite fundamental. I am tempted simply to say 'QED' – case proven – and to end here: all the emphasis which has been given to the idea of social capital as the 'missing link' or as a crucially important analytical tool is misplaced; and it has been shown up for what it is – a blind which obscures the struggles for democracy. 'Community development', albeit gift-wrapped in the currently fashionable rhetoric of social capital, is no more feasible now than it was fifty years ago in the context of an undemocratic society founded on high levels of inequality. What emerges as being crucially important is 'a process of democratization', though what this might entail is not addressed – and certainly not the possibility that it might require redistributive political struggle (to achieve land reform, for example). Enrique Pantoja, like the authors of the Rowntree Foundation study, or Anthony Bebbington, battles gamely on to support the notion that the idea of social capital is somehow a great discovery, opening up new possibilities, but no more than them is he able to persuade the reader that it adds anything, or that it is anything other than a very convenient screen.

8

Conclusion

The Case for Political Action

Only a few years ago the whole idea of 'social capital' was unheard of outside a small circle of professional sociologists. But since about 1995 it has come to be the subject of a great deal of academic enthusiasm in the United States and in Britain, and it has even been declared the 'missing link' in development theory by the World Bank. The extraordinary rise of the idea is due especially to the work of Robert Putnam, first on Italy and later on his native United States, published from 1993 onwards. In this research Putnam claimed to have demonstrated that there are strong causal connections between the existence of 'civic engagement', reflected in such things as high levels of newspaper readership and – especially – the existence of lots of voluntary associations (like sports clubs, music groups or bird watchers' societies), and outcomes that can be labelled as 'good governance'. Putnam's research and 'discoveries' have been the subjects of detailed criticism (and refutation) by serious students of Italian and of US social history. Nevertheless, they were pressed into the service of a view that had started to become fashionable in the early 1990s. This was that 'civil society', understood to mean the sphere of association situated between state on the one hand, and family and kin groups on the other – or even more simplistically as 'NGOs' – is both a condition for good government *and* capable of standing very substantially in place of the state. In the context of the popularity of neo-liberal ideas – that states are inherently predatory, bureaucrats inevitably rent-seekers, and politicians always venal pursuers of power-in-order-to-secure-profits – then the notion that 'citizens' could so much better look after themselves through association in civil society was of course immensely attractive. Never mind that the non-governmental organizations which have been more or less equated with 'civil society' are not democratically accountable (or, at least, only rarely so).[1] How much better for health services, or schools, or water supply and sanitation services, to be run by citizens for themselves, or perhaps with the assistance of the increasingly ubiquitous NGOs, rather than for them to be the responsibility of states! Development agencies should therefore aim to fund these organizations rather than states or their agencies. The voluntary associations, after all, are – aren't they? – the effective instruments of 'participation' and of 'empowerment', not political parties or labour unions or political mass movements. Putnam's work seemed to provide the strongest possible scholarly justification for and backing of this whole set of ideas. My purpose in this book, on the other hand, has been to show just how *weak* is Putnam's theorization of social capital, and how flawed the reasoning that supports this whole gamut of ideas about civil society and NGOs. It successfully supports the systematic depoliticization of development (which is, of course, in itself a deeply political act) by occluding the recognition of power and of class relations. 'Social capital', I have argued, is an additional weapon in the armoury of the 'anti-politics machine' constituted by the discourses and practices of 'development'; and the upshot of my critique of the concept is to reassert the centrality of political action in progressive social transformation.

The main findings of the book can be summarized fairly quickly:

1. The idea of 'social capital' that has exploded across the social sciences, and across many areas of public policy over the last five years or so, has been encouraged most influentially by the World Bank. This has come about even though there remains a great deal of confusion over exactly what the term means. The confusion may even have been a source of strength because it has meant that it has been possible for the idea to be picked up and used in a wide variety of ways. It is a convenient hanger for many

agendas, or, as two World Bank writers have themselves put it, 'Social capital, while not all things to all people, is many things to many people.'[2] Above all, and most strikingly in the way in which it has been elaborated within the Bank, it has proven itself so attractive because it has quite systematically obscured class politics and power.

2. We might almost argue that if the idea of social capital had not already had some currency in the academic literature by the beginning of the 1990s it would have had to have been invented. This is because it answers so well to the development policy agenda of the 1990s, which was concerned with what makes for 'good government', very largely in response to the perceived failures of the strict neo-liberalism of (roughly speaking) the 1980s. This has opened up a new space for consideration of 'non-economic factors' in development. At the same time currents of thought in institutional and in information-theoretic economics have drawn attention to the importance of information and, in its absence, of trust, to which social capital seems to speak. Further, the idea of social capital resonates with the communitarian agenda which has been politically very fashionable in the West. 'Getting the social relations right' is the call of the times. But 'getting the social relations right' is also a dangerous slogan – after all, it might be understood to mean that the social relations of production need to be changed. Social capital has proven to be a valuable idea because it seems to be a way of talking about 'changing social relations' – but without seriously questioning existing power relations and property rights.

3. In attempts to explain the meaning of social capital there is often recourse to metaphor. It is the 'glue' that holds society together. Elsewhere social capital is understood as meaning 'resources that people have by virtue of the social relationships in which they are involved'. In either case it would seem that all societies have social capital, by definition. Commonly, social capital is defined in a more restricted sense, as referring specifically to social networks and to horizontal/voluntary/local associations; and it is thought both that there are measurable differences between societies in these respects (or even in terms of values, specifically levels of trust) , and that it can be shown that there is a strong positive correlation between social capital in this sense, and various desirable outputs – incomes, health, better-functioning schools

and democracy ('health, wealth and wisdom'). Moreover, it seems that these organizational resources can even compensate or substitute for financial and physical resources – particularly those that might be generated through or organized by the state. Even more, therefore, has the idea recommended itself to the World Bank, as it has to the conservative right in the United States.

4. Robert Putnam's research on social capital in the United States is exemplary. It seems to demonstrate a causal connection between participation in 'horizontal associations' in American society and civic engagement, and desirable developmental outcomes, and it implies that people can lift themselves up by their own bootstraps – if only they have, or can build, such social capital. The research also shows strong correlations geographically and historically between social capital, thus defined, with levels of equality/inequality in American society. Yet Putnam himself does not even entertain the conclusion that perhaps policies to improve income equality would enhance community governance. Instead his own conclusions for action resonate with deeply conservative, communitarian and anti-statist sentiments in the United States, and suggest such measures only as reforms to the Scout Movement, or seeking to ensure that 'by 2010 (we) Americans will spend less time travelling and more time connected with our neighbours'.

5. On the basis of demonstrations of the efficacy of social capital (the most influential being those of Putnam on Italy and America, and of Narayan and Pritchett using survey data from Tanzania), it has sometimes been suggested that 'abundant social capital' (or what is more or less the same thing, if social capital is taken to mean local associations, a 'vibrant civil society' – as this has come to be understood in the development discourse), is a condition for 'good government' and successful economic development. Both logically and historically, such an argument about the direction of causality is clearly wrong, when such associations depend upon the existence of a framework of laws that commands authority. The further point here is that there is no reason to believe that trust developed through interpersonal relations (as in local associations) is simply aggregated up into societal trust. The relationship may well run in the opposite direction (some empirical research suggests 'a stronger relationship running from trust in institutions to interpersonal trust than the

other way round, suggesting that more trustworthy governmental institutions make for greater social trust in a society'). But the emphasis in the social capital literature on the causal primacy of *specifically non-political* social networks and local associations suggests that it is possible to have effective democracy without the inconveniences of contestational politics. The idea of social capital depoliticizes development. Further still, therefore, has the idea recommended itself to the World Bank. For 'developers' from agencies like the Bank, politics is awkward, since it so often seems to stand in the way of 'rationally' derived solutions to problems.[3]

6. It is quite clear that social capital in this particular sense of horizontal/voluntary/local association is a two-edged sword. There is a 'dark side' with several aspects. First, there is obviously a whole range of strong associations – mafias, gangs, cartels and the like – which are anti-social, and detrimental to the needs and interests of the society as a whole. Secondly, 'one person's social capital is another person's social exclusion'. Strong groups are often characterized by exclusivism, and in circumstances in which there are few cross-cutting links between such strong groups then it is perfectly possible that 'high levels of social capital' will be associated with conflict.

7. It has thus been recognized (belatedly, it has to be said) that social capital (understood in this particular way), like 'civil society' when this is understood to mean the sphere of voluntary association that exists between state and family and kinship groups, exists in a field of power. It is perfectly possible for resource-poor groups of people to have strong social networks, but that these deliver little. Or as Beall puts it, it may be that 'the poor have weak bonds which while providing some semblance of security in times of need, serve to exclude them from broader social processes'. Social capital is therefore both contextual, and an aspect of the differentiation of classes (as Bourdieu argued in his work, the first substantial exposition of the idea of social capital, which is very largely ignored by the social capitalists of the World Bank).

8. This recognition has led to the suggestion (intended to 'save' social capital from the criticisms summarized in points 5 and 6 above), that it is important to distinguish between 'bonding capital' ('ties that give communities a sense of identity and common

purpose') and 'bridging capital' (the 'ties that transcend various social divides'). Both are necessary for 'good government' and all the rest. Latterly, a third type or variant of social capital has been added: 'linking capital', which connects poor or subordinated people and, it is suggested, individuals in positions of power and influence. Or it may be used to refer to the role that individuals can play in facilitating access to information or resources for groups of poorer people These distinctions perhaps represent an advance upon the earlier understanding of 'social capital' as being more or less equivalent to local/voluntary/horizontal association, but in the way in which they have been presented they systematically ignore class and power relations. Indicative of this is the fact that no mention is made of avowedly political organizations, such as – notably – political parties or trade unions, in any of the discussion. Yet in cases that appear in the social capital literature in which there is evidence of the existence of 'ties that transcend various social divides' and of 'linking capital' – such as in Kerala – the role of these political organizations in creating a sense of common citizenship, transcending 'bonded communities', is unmistakable. As Patrick Heller argues in his work on Kerala, 'A high degree of associationalism in and of itself cannot explain the structural transformations that have underscored Kerala's social development . . . It has entailed a fundamental realignment in the balance of class forces.' This came about as a result of class-based political action, of which there is no reflection at all in the 'policy literature' that advocates the construction of 'bridging' and 'linking capital'.

9. The depoliticizing rhetoric of 'social capital' is further made manifest in the general neglect in this 'policy literature' of the research of Peter Evans, Judith Tendler and others (including Heller). Their work, emanating as it does from some of the leading American universities, receives due recognition in the World Bank – but only superficially, perhaps because it draws such strong attention to what one writer has described as the 'rawer' questions of political economy. Evans et al. analyse the synergy that can arise in social relationships across 'the public–private divide', between state agencies and citizens – which is more or less equivalent to what Putnam describes as the 'virtuous circle' linking civic engagement and good government. But whereas Putnam ascribes this virtuous circle to historic endowments of

social capital, Evans and his fellow researchers show that the possibility of its arising depends upon the existence of coherent state institutions and of rule-based political competition, usually in the context of relatively egalitarian social structures: 'If egalitarian societies with robust public bureaucracies provide the most fertile ground for synergistic state-society relations, most of the Third World offers arid prospects.' Their attempts subsequently to moderate the bluntness of this conclusion are not altogether successful (as I showed in chapter 5).

10. What are we to make of the evasiveness of the policy pronouncements of the World Bank on social capital with regard to the political and distributional questions which are so clearly involved (as they are in the US case, even according to Putnam's own findings)? After all, even one of the papers in the World Bank's Social Capital initiative – that on community development in the Orissa coalfield – concludes that recognition of power relations must enter into any evaluation of social capital, and implies, at least, that without redistribution social capital offers little or nothing. One possible interpretation of the evasiveness which is shown on the Social Capital website and in the *World Development Report 2000/2001* is that the idea of social capital is being used as a kind of 'Trojan Horse' by progressive social scientists in the Bank itself, to challenge the mainstream development agenda and perhaps even the hegemony exercized in the Bank by neo-classical economists who are usually sympathetic to neo-liberal ideas. It is possible that, as it were, by 'speaking to power' in the language that power (in this case the Bank economists) understands (the language of 'capital' but in the phrasing of rational choice), the power-holders can be persuaded to change their thinking and their ways. Perhaps. But another interpretation is that the social capitalists in the Bank have wittingly or unwittingly dumbed-down these ideas in stripping them of the potentially radical implications that are brought out by Evans, Heller and others. Certainly the critical edge of the concept of social capital in the work of Pierre Bourdieu has been blunted, and in the way in which it is presented by the Bank's social capitalists it both reflects and reinforces the hegemony of a style of social science – dominated by methodological individualism and rational choice theorizing – that evades problems to do with class and power. In the ways in which it is used by the Bank's

social capitalists, the idea of social capital plays a useful part in the anti-politics machine, rather than constituting a 'Trojan Horse' to challenge the orthodoxy of the Washington consensus. When we dance with the powerful in order to 'influence them', we must always ask who is being influenced – and remind ourselves of the challenge in the song from Harlan County: 'Which side are you on?'

Concluding observations

In the contemporary discourse on development articulated in international agencies, notably the World Bank, there is a good deal of emphasis upon the virtues of 'participation' – sometimes also taken as implying 'empowerment' – and upon 'decentralization', which is seen either as the key means of realizing participation or sometimes as being more or less equivalent to it. These three buzz-words are used in close alliance with the two others, 'social capital' and 'civil society', that have been discussed in this book. These ideas are painted as being 'progressive' and are deceptively attractive. They are attractive because they imply active support for the ideas and the needs and the aspirations of the common people. Can one possibly be 'against' participation and empowerment? But these ideas are deceptive because they are used to veil the nature and the effects of power, and – as I have argued in this book – they hold out the prospects of democracy (in 'civil society') without the inconveniences of contestational politics and of the conflicts of ideas and interests that are an essential part of democracy.

It is most significant that the concept of 'civil society' as it is used in this discourse excludes 'political society'; and that the sorts of 'voluntary local associations' that are endorsed are not *political* organizations (such as political parties or trade unions), but are rather – when they are not choirs, football clubs and the like – what are described as 'non-governmental organizations'. These are not organizations that are democratically accountable, as even their partisans recognize. Michael Edwards and David Hulme, who have convened several major international conferences of NGO activists, concede that 'there is increasing evidence that NGOs and grass-roots organizations do not perform as effectively as [has] been assumed in terms of poverty-reach, cost-effectiveness, sustainability, popular participation (including gender), flexibility and innovation', and – as avowed partisans – they recognize that NGOs must address the problems surrounding their democratic accountability, and their relations to the political process.[4] For these authors, realization of the potentials of non-governmental and of grass-roots organizations really depends on getting over the notion that they constitute a 'magic bullet'. That civil society exists in a field of power – or that there are differences of power within civil society – hardly seems to cross the minds of those who wish to see the space of civil society expanded, and that of the state (and perhaps of the market) reduced. The discourse is in fact quite deliberately apolitical, in a way that is ultimately supportive of neo-liberal orthodoxy.

'Civility' or 'civicness' (which is how Putnam also talks about 'civic engagement', in his version synonymous with 'social capital') actually implies notions of impartiality of treatment and of the equality of individuals as citizens before the law. The concept of 'civil society', too (and there are, of course, a number of different conceptualizations of the idea) implies the existence of laws and of less formal codes for conduct (such as ideas of 'professional ethics'). It is when people generally believe in the legitimacy of these institutions, and are reasonably confident that the values and norms that inhere within them will motivate those who are concerned in implementing them, that civicness/civil society flourishes, and there is a fair degree of generalized societal trust – as Putnam actually states, ironically enough, in his discussion of the history of civic organization in Italy. But it is not at all clear logically, nor demonstrable empirically, that these conditions *arise* from the existence of horizontal, voluntary associations. The existence of civil society, therefore, and of generalized trust in a society, presuppose an institutional framework put into place through the agency of a state. Arguments about civic engagement = social capital = voluntary associations are flawed logically and, as historians of Italy have shown with regard to Putnam's work, historically false. The conclusion that has been derived, therefore, to the effect that the existence of a 'vibrant civil society' or of 'abundant stocks of social capital' – both being equated with 'lots of voluntary associations' – is a condition for functioning democracy and/or 'good government', is both logically and historically doubtful. It is wrong to suppose that 'social capital is something that arises or declines in a realm apart from politics and government'.[5]

The idea of social capital – which is the one that has been so influential – deriving from Putnam's work, is confused, and the 'big idea' associated with it, that voluntary associations are the 'missing link' in development, is misleading. But it is not just confused and misleading, it is also a pernicious idea. It is not an accident that Putnam's views of social capital in America have been picked up so enthusiastically by conservatives, even though Putnam describes himself as a 'progressive'. Part of the enthusiasm for 'constructing social capital' and 'building civil society' is that these ideas are consistent with the neo-liberal agenda of reducing the role of the state, partly in order to make possible large cuts in public expenditure. A good deal of the policy literature on social capital reflects the idea of 'people pulling themselves together from below without much help from government or their privileged fellow citizens' – which is very convenient for those who benefit from cuts in social expenditure.

These critical reflections upon the popular conception of social capital derived from Putnam also help to make the case for political action that does address problems of distribution, of class and of power. The major threads in the evidence and argument that I have reviewed in this book are these:

> *While all societies have the sorts of resources which have been labelled as 'stocks of social capital', the implications or the 'value' of these resources is entirely contextually dependent.

> *Local organization or community action on their own are liable to be ineffectual, or to be vehicles for the interests of more powerful people, in the absence of significant external linkages, especially (even if not exclusively) through political organizations.

> *Civil society is established in relation to institutions that are defined by the state.

> *Arguments (i) which call for 'participation'/ 'community action'/ 'action in civil society' in isolation from or as an

alternative to state action; or (*ii*) which more or less equate these with 'decentralization', and take that to mean the withdrawal of the state at the centre; or (*iii*) which suggest that 'stocks of social capital'/ 'vibrant civil society' are conditions for the establishment of effective democracy and 'good government', are misleading – and it is quite misleading to suggest that 'social capital', understood to mean 'local voluntary association', is the key condition for 'health, wealth, wisdom and happiness' (i.e 'development') in a population.

★The realization of the potentials of participative, community-level action depends upon the establishment of a political context that secures the rights of less advantaged or less 'resource-full' people, often against local power-holders; and which creates conditions for the existence of deliberative democracy. (This is the powerful conclusion drawn from the study of the Orissa coalfields outlined in chapter 7).

★The successful realization of the potentials of participative, community-level action also involves networks among actors at different levels and in different sites, including especially local organizations, political parties and state agencies, as well, perhaps, as NGOs and social movement organizations.

These conclusions are borne out in the experience of the People's Campaign in Kerala.

Public action, and deepening democracy: the People's Campaign for Decentralized Planning in Kerala

The way in which devolution to local bodies has worked in Kerala since the inauguration of the People's Campaign for Decentralized Planning in 1996 shows up these conclusions in sharp relief. The Left Front government took the bold step of devolving responsibility for a large share (35–40 per cent) of plan expenditure to local bodies; in advance, too, of the restructuring of the bureaucracy which is often held to be a precondition for decentralization. The state government then also intervened actively to assist local people in identifying opportunities and constraints, often through encouraging the activities of volunteers like those – notably – of the Kerala Sastra Sahitya Parishad (KSSP, the People's Science Movement) who have been involved in facilitating local resource mapping, and in providing training in project planning. This seems, incidentally, to be one instance (and how abundant are such cases?) in which the principles of Participatory Rural Appraisal have been put into practice, rather than remaining in the realm of rhetoric.[6] There is some evidence that in this case PRA has helped to catalyse increased participation and associational activity at the grass roots – as it is supposed to, according to the philosophy underlying it – but in a context, clearly, in which the use of these techniques has been facilitated through interventions of the government.

There is a three-way dynamic, therefore, between local and central government, and civil society, that is politically articulated. The presence of members of the KSSP on the State Planning Board shows the possibility of the influence of a civil society organization at the central as well as at the local level, exactly as Tendler found in Ceara; while NGOs provide inputs into locally conceived plans (though not invariably so – NGOs in some instances have been setting up parallel structures and projects, which may in the end weaken the efforts of the local bodies). There is an element, too, of the 'magic' worked by 'distrust' between central and local government in the procedures which have been instituted for subjecting local plans to expert, as well as to democratic, scrutiny, albeit in a way that involves local volunteers and not just staff from the line departments of the state government. And the whole experiment is underlaid – it cannot be stressed too much – by the prior accomplishment of land reform in Kerala. Inequalities persist in local society, of course, but local power has been contained through land reform in Kerala, and the rights of less 'resource-full' people have been secured – by the state, of course – to a much greater extent than they have been elsewhere in the country.

Only time will tell whether Kerala's experiment with democratic decentralization will yield the sorts of results in terms of production and productivity which the late E M S Namboodiripad sought when he started it off. But there is no doubt that it has increased 'participation', in the sense that it has involved more people in decision-making about matters of public concern. What is especially remarkable about it is the way in which planning has been used as a means of encouraging participation and social mobilization. Perhaps it has drawn on existing 'social capital' in neighbourhoods and communities (which might help to account for some of the differences that have appeared between parts of the state). Equally arguably, it has been responsible for 'constructing social capital', and because of this, through the way in which it has drawn people in to what are clearly 'civic endeavours', it has 'consolidated civil society'. But it has all taken place in the context of a political process in which different groups of actors at different social levels are all involved with the state, not by 'constructing-social capital-as-local-organizations' and thereby 'consolidating civil society' in place of politically directed state action.[7]

The Kerala story constitutes a powerful statement, therefore, against the currently fashionable ideas about 'social capital' and 'civil society' that have been the subject of this book. Isaac and Franke write, 'The role of *political society* in both the state-centred and/or civil-society-led paradigms explaining the decentralization process, is conspicuous by its absence . . . But in a situation such as Kerala's, which is characterized by an active political society with hegemonic positions held by Left political formations, political society holds the key to democratic decentralization.' Here, it is not the 'social capital' that lies in the congeries of voluntary associations highlighted by Robert Putnam – including choirs, bowling leagues, football teams and the like – that counts, but rather powerful class and mass organizations (which in Kerala encompass nearly one third of the adult population). The People's Campaign has involved public action, and the interplay between government and people's organizations, in the context of a political process. The same – *pace* Putnam – seems to have held in Italy, where the PCI fostered civic engagement, and it is likely to hold elsewhere, too.

Notes

1 INTRODUCTION

1 Tarrow 1996, p. 396.
2 This definition comes from Putnam's book *Making Democracy Work: civic traditions in modern Italy* (Princeton, NJ: Princeton University Press, 1993, p. 167).
3 This is the headline used in an issue of a UK-based publication 'Development Research Insights' (September 2000), reporting on a set of papers dealing with 'the economic analysis of social capital'. This publication is accessible through the website: www.id21.org.
4 Christiaan Grootaert, a Senior Economist, author of the chapter entitled 'Social Capital: The Missing Link?', in *Expanding the Measure of Wealth – Indicators of Environmentally Sustainable Development* (Washington DC: World Bank 1997).
5 The idea of 'the anti-politics machine' comes from the work of an anthropologist, James Ferguson. It appears in the title of his book, *The Anti-Politics Machine: 'Development', Depoliticization and Bureaucratic Power in Lesotho* (Cambridge and New York, Cambridge University Press, 1990; reissued in 1994: Minneapolis and London, University of Minnesota Press). The book explains quite brilliantly how apparently 'failed' development projects serve the interests of power; and how *'By uncompromisingly reducing poverty to a technical problem, and by promising technical solutions to the sufferings of powerless and oppressed people, the hegemonic problematic of 'development' is the principal means through which the problem of poverty is depoliticised in the world today'*.
6 'Stuff used to produce things' is the definition of capital given in *The Pocket Economist*, published by *The Economist* newspaper (see Pennant-Rea and Emmott 1983).
7 Hart 1988.
8 My phrasing here leaves open the possibility that 'social capital' refers to the 'resources' (of trust and reciprocity) or the networks which give rise to them, or indeed to the combination of social structure/networks and the ideas and values associated with them. The literature on

social capital is shot through with ambiguity as to which position is to be preferred. Foley and Edwards (1999) discuss this critical issue in an important review of research, and conclude that the term 'social capital' has come to refer more specifically only to associational life or social networks, rather than social norms as such.

9 Bourdieu's point is brought out very clearly in research by sociologists on *'la grande bourgeoisie'* in France. Pincon and Pincon-Charlot, for example, writing in *Le Monde Diplomatique* for September 2001, and describing the life-style of the great bourgeois families, refer to world cruises as *'hauts lieux de gestion du capital social'* ['pinnacles in the formation of social capital']. They note that 'Entering the great bourgeoisie is accomplished through the accumulation of wealth. But this is not sufficient in itself. It takes time to build up the network of social relationships that is the guarantee of social standing.'

10 Narayan and Pritchett 1997, abstract.

11 Mosse 1994.

12 Grootaert 1997.

13 On this point see, for example, Gordon et al. 1982, on the United States, and Harriss, Kannan and Rodgers 1990 for an Indian example.

14 Olson 1982.

15 The expression appears in the title of a paper of James Putzel's, though it was apparently first used by Elinor Ostrom. See Putzel 1997.

16 This quotation and those which follow in this paragraph from the *World Development Report 2000/2001* (World Bank 2000, p. 128).

17 See for example Paul Brass's book *Theft of an Idol* (1997) on the role of the police in North India; and Jeffrey and Lerche 2000.

18 Indeed the best analysis that I have yet seen of this kind, in unpublished work by Peter Mayer of the Department of Politics in the University of Adelaide, does show that Kerala (by a street) tops the list of major states on a 'civic community index' *à la* Putnam.

19 Dreze and Sen 1989.

20 The answer to this rhetorical question is 'no'. Those who need to be convinced of this may consult Ramachandran 1996, or Patrick Heller's book *The Labor of Development* (1999).

21 It is interesting that in French the same word may be used to refer both to 'politics' and to 'policy': *'la politique'*. Maybe the French language recognizes an identity which the English language tends to obscure?

22 The impossibility of a 'self-regulating market economy' and the dependence of this idea on the fictions that land, labour (= people), and money are commodities is the subject of Karl Polanyi's classic *The Great Transformation* (1944).

23 The writer of the song, Florence Reece, was the wife of a union organizer in Harlan County. She wrote the lyrics a few days after her home

was ransacked by armed men who were looking for her husband, men from the 'security forces' who were enforcing the wishes of the mining company as law. See Couto 1999, pp. 1–6.

2 WHERE THE 'MISSING LINK' CAME FROM

1   Putnam 1993, p. 181.
2   Putnam 1993.
3   I owe this information to Ben Fine. See Fine 2001, p. 83.
4   Putnam 2000.
5   Tarrow 1967; 1994.
6   Banfield 1958.
7   When Edward Banfield put arguments from which Putnam draws some inspiration he needed a police escort in the United States, while Putnam conversely, is positively feted. See Fine 2001, chapter 6.
8   Woolcock traces the antecedents of the idea from the philosophers of the Scottish Enlightenment: 1998.
9   This and the previous quotation from Putnam 2000, p. 19.
10 Moser 1996, p. 96 n. 7.
11 Jacobs 1961.
12 I have not checked this assertion with complete scrupulousness, but I believe that is only Woolcock's article (1998) which has even a mention of Bourdieu's name and work.
13 One of the principal exponents of this is of course the Nobel prize-winning economist, Gary Becker. Becker has also sought to theorize social capital. For a critical commentary see Fine 2001, chapter 3.
14 The way in which Bourdieu's social capital has passed 'from distinction to extinction' is elucidated by Fine 2001, chapter 4.
15 Coleman 1990.
16 Coleman 1990, p. 37.
17 It is found in Coleman, 1988 (which may be accessed via the World Bank's Social Capital Homepage); and 1990, chapter 12.
18 Coleman 1990, p. 300.
19 This is in Coleman 1988.
20 Coleman 1990, p. 302.
21 Coleman 1990, p. 303.
22 Coleman 1990, p. 304.
23 Rudner 1994, p. 234.
24 I am reminded of a practical (albeit functionalist) explanation of why it was that a group of Australian Aborigines celebrated a religious festival on a massive scale during a period of drought. The festival, because it brought together large numbers of people, constituted a mechanism for the communication of lots of information.

25 It is what Stiglitz (formerly Chief Economist in the World Bank) calls 'information-theoretic economics'. See Fine 2000, chapter 1, for critical commentary.
26 Coleman 1990, p. 317.
27 Coleman 1990, p. 313.
28 I am guilty myself of having misrepresented the significance of Bourdieu's conception in an earlier publication. See Harriss and de Renzio 1997.
29 Bourdieu 1993, pp. 32–3. Other sources on Bourdieu's thinking on social capital include: Bourdieu 1980; 1986; 1987 and Bourdieu and Wacquant 1992. I also describe social capital as 'connections' in chapter 1 of this book.
30 This and the previous quotations, and points made here from Fine 2001, p. 117, and chapter 4.
31 Putnam 1993, p. 157.
32 Putnam 1993, p. 89.
33 Putnam 1993, p. 90.
34 Putnam 1993, p. 94.
35 Putnam 1990, p. 114.
36 Bevilacqua, cited by Putnam 1993, p. 143.
37 Professor Geof Wood, University of Bath, March 1999 pers.comm.
38 Banfield 1958.
39 Putnam 1993, p. 178.
40 Putnam 1993, p. 180.
41 e.g. North 1990.
42 Putnam 1993, 183.
43 This and the previous quotation from Putnam 1993, p. 184.
44 Putnam 1993, p. 181.
45 Putnam 1993, p. 174.
46 The reference is to Granovetter 1973; but see also Granovetter's seminal article of 1985.
47 Putnam 1993, p. 175.
48 Putnam 1995, n. 2.
49 Putnam 1993, p. 170.
50 Putnam 1996.
51 Couto 1999, p. 4.

3 THE FRAGILITY OF THE FOUNDATIONS

1 From Tarrow 1996.
2 I am reminded of the words of the historian Eric Stokes: 'The science of history proceeds no doubt as the detailed criticism of sociological generalisations, but of generalisations so rudimentary and so little

analysed that they constitute primitive archetypal images . . . rather than a formed system of ideas.' (Stokes 1978, p. 19).

3   According to Sabetti, for example, Putnam is 'insensitive to the anti-feudal (and anti-Spanish) bias that has marked much of the literature on south Italy since the eighteenth century' (1996, p. 25). But Putnam is in good company. Weber's view of the 'protestant ethic' was rooted in popular thinking about the characters of 'protestants' and 'catholics' in mid-nineteenth-century Germany.

4   Tarrow 1996, p. 392 (nn. 13, 14).

5   David 1985.

6   Tarrow notes that *Making Democracy Work* was greeted by one reviewer as 'a stunning breakthrough in political culture research' and remarks that if the book 'is not a cultural interpretation, then Putnam and his collaborators' fooled him too. (1996, p. 390 n. 7)

7   Sadly, the conceptualization of 'culture' in a recent collection on *Culture Matters: How Values Shape Human Progress*, edited by Lawrence E Harrison and Samuel P Huntington (2000), that seems to have become influential in the United States, is one that fails to take account of these more critical views of the meaning of the term.

8   Sabetti 1996, p. 23.

9   This point is made both by Goldberg 1996; and by Sabetti 1996.

10   This, and the succeeding quotations in this paragraph, come from Rotberg's introduction to the *Journal of Interdisciplinary History* collection; Rotberg 1999.

11   Indeed, this is the impression which is given even in tolerably informative travel guides to Italy!

12   Tarrow 1996, p. 393.

13   This and other points in this paragraph from Sabetti 1996.

14   The contemporary Italian accounts of the 'iron circle' are strikingly comparable with those of agrarian relations in many parts of India in the present.

15   Tarrow 1996, p. 395.

16   Tarrow 1996, p. 394.

17   Mayer 2001, p. 5.

18   Quotations from Putzel 1997.

19   Quotations here from Putnam 1993, p. 119.

20   Goldberg 1996.

21   The title of his book: Saberwal 1996.

22   Levi 1996, p. 49.

23   Levi 1996, p. 48.

24   Platteau 1994; Moore 1994.

25   This research is cited by Foley and Edwards 1999.

26   Cohen 1999, p. 223.

27 Levi 1996, p. 51.
28 Cohen 1999, p. 220.
29 And that is, indeed, explicit in classic notions of what constitutes 'civil society'. John Keane, summing up his extensive explorations of the older literature on civil society', says: 'Civil society . . . is an ideal-typical category that both describes and envisages a complex and dynamic ensemble of legally protected non-governmental institutions that tend to be non-violent, self-organizing, self-reflexive, and permanently in tension with each other and with *the state institutions that 'frame', constrict and enable their activities.'* (Keane 1998, p. 6; emphasis mine)
30 This and the preceding quotation from Cohen 1999, pp. 220–1.
31 This and the preceding quotation from Levi 1996, pp. 51–2.

4 'ANTI-POLITICS' IN AMERICA

1 Quotation from an article by Nicholas Lemann in *The Atlantic Monthly*, April 1996.
2 This is in Putnam 1993a.
3 Putnam 2000.
4 See Putnam 1993a.
5 Putnam 1995.
6 Lemann 1996.
7 Putnam 1996.
8 Putnam 1996.
9 The debate can be accessed through a website: www.epn.org/issues/civilsociety.html.
10 Samuelson; accessed via the website referred to above: see n. 9.
11 Lemann 1996.
12 Sirianni and Friedland 1995, pp. 12–13. This article is accessible from the website of the Civic Practices Network in the US: www.cpn.org.
13 Sirianni and Friedland 1995, p. 15.
14 Such synergy is the theme of the next chapter.
15 A full statement by Senator Coats can be found on the website referred to above: n. 9.
16 These and subsequent quotations from Skocpol 1996.
17 See her contributions to *Civic Engagement in American Democracy;* Fiorina and Skocpol 1999.
18 Skocpol et al., n.d., p. 7.
19 There were 74 post offices for every 100,000 inhabitants compared with 17 in Britain and only four in France. See Skocpol et al., n.d., p. 22.
20 Quotation from a summary by Rotberg 1999, p. 350.
21 From Skocpol 1996.

22 Putnam 2000.
23 Putnam made this point when he responded to critics in *The American Prospect* in 1996.
24 Willis 2000.
25 Cohen 1999, p. 226, citing Schudson 1996.
26 The use of mobile phones was a key factor in the (anti-democratic) mobilization of a disparate collection of road hauliers and farmers in the UK in September 2000, against the government, over the level of taxes on fuel.
27 Putnam 2000, p. 254. The passage continues: 'The core of this civic generation is the cohort born 1925–1930, who attended grade school during the Great Depression, spent World War II in high school (or on the battlefield), first voted in 1948 or 1952, set up housekeeping in the 1950s, and saw their first television when they were in the late twenties. Since polling began, this cohort has been exceptionally civic . . .'
28 Putnam 2000, p. 294.
29 Peter Mayer's work on social capital in Italy and in India shows how levels of female literacy in Italy in the 1870s strongly predict variations in the later strength of 'civic community' in that country, as measured by Putnam (Mayer 2000; and see chapter 3 of this book).
30 See figures 92 and 93 in Putnam 2000, pp. 360–1.
31 This and the previous quotation from Putnam 2000, p. 359.
32 Bowles 1999, p. 9.
33 This and the preceding quotation from Putnam 1996a; but see also Putnam 2000, p. 413.
34 Putnam 2000, p. 399.
35 This is the final chapter of *Bowling Alone* (Putnam 2000).
36 Quotations from Putnam 2000, chapter 24.
37 This quotation, and the argument here, come from the 'Conclusion' of Richard Couto's fine book *Making Democracy Work Better* (Couto 1999).

5 SOCIAL CAPITAL AND 'SYNERGY ACROSS THE PUBLIC–PRIVATE DIVIDE'

1 Evans 1996a, p. 1122.
2 Heller 1996, p. 1057. See also Heller 1999.
3 The collection was published in the journal *World Development*, vol. 24, no. 6, July 1996 (Evans 1996); but I include also the work of Judith Tendler of the Massachusetts Institute of Technology, who was a contributor to the seminar from which the *World Development* collection derived, though not to the collection itself. I refer to her book *Good Government in the Tropics* (published in 1997).

4 Evans 1996a, pp. 1124–5.
5 These quotations from Evans 1996a, p. 1129.
6 These are studies respectively by Lam, Heller, Ostrom, Fox and Burawoy, in Evans 1996; and the work of Judith Tendler on Ceara state in northeast Brazil (see Tendler 1997).
7 Evans 2000 (a paper presented at the International Conference on Democratic Decentralization held in Thiruvananthapuram in May 2000).
8 This is demonstrated in Lam's study in Evans 1996. But see also my own research in Sri Lanka: Harriss 1977.
9 Moore 1989, cited by Evans 1996a, p. 1121.
10 See especially Evans 1995.
11 Evans 1992, p. 174.
12 Evans' argument may or may not be right. It is possible that things have changed in India since he did his research (before the introduction of the economic reform programme in 1991). My concern here is to illustrate a general argument.
13 See Tendler 1997.
14 Evans' description (1996a, p. 1121).
15 Evans 1996a, p. 1122.
16 Evans 1996a, p. 1124.
17 The argument, for example, of writers like Lloyd and Susanne Rudolph 1987.
18 Evans 1996a, p. 1125. Swaminathan S Anklesaria Aiyar's ideas about caste-based development for India take no account of these problems.
19 Heller 1996, p. 1057.
20 Judith Tendler refers critically to this 'fever' in her 1997 *Good Government in the Tropics*.
21 Crook and Sverisson 1999.
22 Evans 2000.

6 SOCIAL CAPITAL IN THE WORLD BANK

1 Ferguson 1990, p. 18.
2 The 'big bang' image is Ben Fine's.
3 Nicholas Stern, now the Chief Economist of the World Bank, writing in 1997 with Francisco Ferreira, notes: 'In analyzing the Bank's influence on development economics it must be recognized that the Bank's size gives it a unique position. The Bank employs around 800 professional economists . . . These resources dwarf those of any university department or research institution working on development economics' (cited by Fine 2001, p. 146). Michael Cernea, for long the senior sociologist in the World Bank, writes of the '50–60 social scientists who

actually practice development anthropology and sociology' in the Bank that it is 'the world's largest group of this kind working in one place' (Fine 2001, p. 151).

4 I acknowledge the influence here of Ben Fine's substantial discussion. See Fine 2001, Chapter 8.

5 See for example Woolcock 1999. His first paper on social capital is a substantial scholarly commentary: see Woolcock 1998.

6 Certainly under its most influential President, Robert McNamara.

7 Lal 1983.

8 The phrase 'the Washington consensus' was suggested by Williamson 1990.

9 Fine 2000, p. 135.

10 A useful source here is Mosley et al., 1991.

11 The most influential criticism of the earlier notion that the Asian Tigers stood testimony to the 'free market' was in Robert Wade's book *Governing the Market* (1990). But World Bank economists resisted these ideas until well into the 1990s (see Wade 1996).

12 One of them, Douglass North, was one of the winners of the Nobel Prize for Economics in 1993.

13 The Bank produced an influential paper on this in April 1992. See World Bank 1992.

14 Stiglitz, cited by Fine 2001, p.139.

15 The preface to the British edition of Etzioni's book *The Spirit of Community* (1995) gives a long list of names of political leaders who have endorsed communitarianism 'although they rarely utter the six-syllable word'.

16 This, and the other quotations in this paragraph, are from Etzioni 1995.

17 This proposition is the subject of an extremely wide-ranging essay, influenced significantly by Putnam, by J-P Platteau, 1994.

18 See Edwards 1999.

19 Cited by Fine 2000, p. 167.

20 See Olson 1982.

21 Narayan 1999, p. 5. Modesty will not forbid me from pointing out that I said this first. See Harriss and de Renzio 1997, p. 926: '"social capital" for some implies "social exclusion for others"' – though the point was made in a comment on work by Portes and Landholt (see the following note).

22 The reference is to Portes and Landholt, 1996.

23 This is the title of the critical article by James Putzel, 1997 (referred to in chapter 1) – which does not appear, incidentally, in the database available on the Bank's Social Capital website.

24 This wording is taken from the description of a paper of Woolcock's as

it is reported in *Development Research Insights* issue number 34 (see chapter 1, n. iii); but it appears in a slightly expanded form in chapter 7 of the World Bank's *World Development Report 2000/2001* (World Bank 2000, p. 128).

25 Beall 2000, p. 16.
26 This and the subsequent quotations from Grootaert, 1997.
27 References are given to Olson 1982; and North, 1990.
28 Fine, 2001, chapter 9.
29 Narayan and Pritchett, 1997 [1996].
30 This quotation from the 'Executive Summary' in Krishna and Uphoff 1999.
31 Their work was used in this way, for example, in the World Bank's *World Development Report 1997,* which was on the theme of 'The State in a Changing World'. See the box on p. 115.
32 Beall 2000, p. 22.
33 World Bank 1975, p. 3.
34 See Bharadwaj 1974, 1985.
35 Including the outstanding earlier work of Ben Fine, or the articles by Harriss and de Renzio, Putzel, Beall and Fox published in an issue of the UK-based *Journal of International Development* in 1997.
36 For evidence on this point see Hodgson and Rothman 1999.

7 PUTTING SOCIAL CAPITAL TO WORK

1 Fine 2001, p. 97.
2 Foley and Edwards 1999; Fine 2001, esp. chapter 7.
3 Morrow 1999.
4 Pantoja 1999, p. 3.
5 Bebbington 1997, 1999; Bebbington and Perreault 1999.
6 Quotations in this paragraph from Bebbington 1997.
7 The reference here is to Granovetter's article on 'The Strength of Weak Ties' (1973), which has been highly influential – not least in the genesis of Woolcock's ideas. Granovetter was led to make the distinction between 'strong' and 'weak' ties in research on access to jobs and labour markets in the USA, when he found that 'weak' ties with rather casual acquaintances were more significant in the ways in which people get into jobs than 'strong' family and kinship connections.
8 Robert Putnam argues that if he had a magic wand which would create more social capital in the USA, he probably wouldn't wave it if it only created more 'bonding' capital (public lecture at the London School of Economics, May 1999).
9 Quotations here are from Woolcock 1999, and from Bebbington 1997.
10 Woolcock 1999 (page numbers not available from web document).

11 Bebbington 1997, p. 194.
12 In Bebbington 1998, and Bebbington and Perreault 1999.
13 Bebbington 1999, p. 2038.
14 Quotations from Joseph Rowntree Foundation, 1998, cited by Cattell and Evans 1999, p. 1.
15 Cattell and Evans 1999.
16 These ideas are reflected in another recent JRF study called *Building Social Capital: self-help in the twenty-first century welfare state* (Mai Wann, n.d.) which is about the rapid expansion in recent years of self-help and mutual aid activities in most Western democracies, and how public funds can usefully support them. Curiously the only place in which the term 'social capital' appears in this particular study is in the title! This is surely a tribute to the perception that 'social capital sells' (since even charitable foundations like to sell their books).
17 This and the preceding quotations in the text from Cattell and Evans 1999, chapter 10.
18 This statement corresponds very closely with the conclusion of the most recent critical treatment of the social capital idea by Foley and Edwards, though it was almost certainly not influenced by these two writers. Foley and Edwards (1999) say: 'Social capital is best conceived as access (networks) plus resources'.
19 I have referred to a draft of the paper dated June 15 1999, which was prepared for the World Conference on Social Capital (referred to on the Social Capital website). It should be possible to download copies – authorship attributed to Pantoja and to Pantelic, his task manager – from the website, though at the time of writing a paper on another subject appears to have been substituted for this one. I know not whether by error or by design.
20 These quotations are from the 'Introduction' in Pantoja 1999.
21 Pantoja 1999, p. 32.
22 Quotations from Pantoja 1999, pp. 38, 44.
23 Quotations from Pantoja 1999, pp. 47, 48, 63–4. With the last statement that I have quoted Pantoja gives as corroborating references Mosse 1994; and Jayaraman and Landjouw 1999.
24 Pantoja's key points are borne out very strikingly in a recent study by Sanjay Kumar and Stuart Corbridge (2001) of another project in eastern India – the 'East India Rainfed Farming Project'. 'The project model is based on a causal theory in which villager participation in planning and development, and the enhancement of villager skills and capacities (along with productivity-enhancing technical innovations) results in sustained improvements in livelihoods'. In practice the project has, according to careful independent evaluation by Kumar and Corbridge, been rather successful in increasing agricultural productivity,

and they have also shown that there is a correlation between the 'social capital' of different individuals, as measured by an index of their social relationships, and agricultural productivity. But who are the people who have most social capital? Unsurprisingly in the context of an inegalitarian, hierarchical society (the notion that the 'tribal societies' of eastern India are homogeneous is a myth), it is those people who are relatively powerful who turn out to have the most social capital. Kumar and Corbridge show that 'the project has been less successful in targeting the poor than richer families have been in targeting the project'. Membership in the development groups set up the EIRFP is biased towards richer and more influential individuals and families, and they have used the groups in order to capture project inputs. This is even expected by members of the poorest families in the villages, while the Project's Community Organizers need to draw on the support of village 'leaders' from amongst the richer and more influential families in order to set up the groups at all. Meanwhile there is evidence in the villages of declining participation in shared labour systems and community grain banks that formerly provided some little security to poorer people. I find this a telling example. Has the EIRFP 'failed', however? As a farming systems project it has, arguably, done pretty well. It has only 'failed' because it has attempted too much or claimed too much for itself. It cannot hope to change the patterns of land ownership and of social exclusion that provide the context for its activities through the attempt to 'build social capital' in development groups. Rather does this attempt tend to reinforce these patterns of inequality and exclusion.

25 The quotations here are from Pantoja 1999, pp. 58–69.

8 CONCLUSION

1 At the time of writing this chapter, the aftermath of the earthquake in Gujarat exposed the pathologies of the 'NGO fix'. Praful Bidwai commented on the way in which 'the elite looks for short-cuts and quick-fixes: for example, NGO assistance, although this cannot be a sustainable substitute for government', while 'a large number of recently formed NGOs stand charged with discrimination against the low castes and religious minorities in the matter of relief distribution' (*Frontline* March 16 2001, p. 121).

2 Narayan and Pritchett 1997 (as previously cited).

3 See Moore and Putzel 1999. It is surely symptomatic that the work done by Moore, Putzel and others, on politics and poverty, should have been encouraged by Ravi Kanbur while he was in charge of the preparation of the World Bank's *World Development Report 2000/2001*,

but that after Kanbur resigned from the Bank, because of internal hostility to some of the ideas in the report, virtually all trace of the Moore–Putzel work was removed.

4 Edwards and Hulme 1995, chapter 1 (quotation p. 6).
5 Skocpol, cited in chapter 4.
6 See Mosse 1994 for a critical treatment of PRA in action in other parts of India.
7 Isaac with Franke 2000.

References

Banfield, E C, 1958, *The Moral Basis of a Backward Society*, Chicago: The Free Press.

Beall, J, 2000, 'Valuing Social Resources or Capitalizing on Them? Social Action and the Limits to Pro-poor Urban Governance, Urban Governance, Partnership and Poverty', Working Paper 19, University of Birmingham.

Bebbington, A, 1997, 'Social Capital and Rural Intensification: Local Organizations and Islands of Sustainability in the Rural Andes', *Geographical Journal*, 163:2, pp. 189–97.

———— 1999, 'Capitals and Capabilities: A Framework for Analyzing Peasant Viability, Rural Livelihoods and Poverty', *World Development*, 27:12, pp. 2021–44.

Bebbington, A and Perreault, T, 1999, 'Social Capital, Development and Access to Resources in Highland Ecuador', *Economic Geography*, 75:4, pp. 395–418.

Bharadwaj, K, 1974, *Production Conditions in Indian Agriculture*, Cambridge: Cambridge University Press.

———— 1985, 'A View on Commercialization in Indian Agriculture and the Development of Capitalism', *Journal of Peasant Studies*, 12:1, pp. 7–25.

Bourdieu, P, 1980, '*Le capital sociale: notes provisoires*', *Actes de la Recherche en Sciences Sociales*, 31, pp. 2–3.

———— 1986, 'The Forms of Capital' in Richardson, J, ed., *Handbook of Theory and Research for the Sociology of Education*, New York: Greenwood Press.

———— 1987, 'What Makes a Social Class? On the Theoretical and Practical Existence of Groups', *Berkeley Journal of Sociology*, XXXII, pp. 1–17.

———— 1993, *Sociology in Question*, London: Sage Publications.

Bourdieu, P and Wacquant, L, 1992, *An Invitation to Reflexive Sociology*, Cambridge: Polity Press.

Bowles, S, 1999, '"Social Capital" and Community Governance', *Focus*, 20:3, Fall (University of Wisconsin–Madison Institute for Research on Poverty), pp. 6–10.

Brass, P, 1997, *Theft of an Idol: Text and Context in the Representation of Collective Violence*, Princeton, NJ: Princeton University Press.

Cattell, V and Evans, M, 1999, *Neighbourhood Images in East London: Social Capital and Social Networks on Two East London Estates*, York: York Publishing Services for the Joseph Rowntree Foundation.

Coleman, J, 1988, 'Social Capital and the Creation of Human Capital', *American Journal of Sociology*, 94: Supplement, pp. S95–S120.

———— 1990, *Foundations of Social Theory*, Cambridge: Harvard University Press.

Cohen, J, 1999, 'Trust, Voluntary Association and Workable Democracy: The Contemporary American Discourse of Civil Society', in Mark E Warren, ed., *Democracy and Trust*, Cambridge: Cambridge University Press.

Couto, R with Catherine S Guthrie, 1999, *Making Democracy Work Better: Mediating Structures, Social Capital and the Democratic Prospect*, Chapel Hill, NC, and London: University of North Carolina Press.

Crook, R and Sverrisson, A, 1999, 'To What Extent Can Decentralized Forms of Government Enhance the Development of Pro-poor Policies and Improve Poverty Alleviation Outcomes?', Working Paper, Institute of Development Studies at the University of Sussex, Brighton UK.

David, P, 1985, 'Clio and the Economics of QWERTY', *American Economic Review*, 75, pp. 332–7.

Dreze, J and Sen, A, 1989, *Hunger and Public Action*, Oxford: Oxford University Press.

Edwards, M, 1999, 'Enthusiasts, Tacticians and Sceptics: The World Bank, Civil Society and Social Capital', World Bank Social Capital Library, Papers in Progress.

Edwards, M and Hulme, D, eds., 1995, *Non-Governmental Organizations – Performance and Accountability, Beyond the Magic Bullet*, London: Earthscan Publications.

Etzioni, A, 1995, *The Spirit of Community: Rights, Responsibilities and the Communitarian Agenda*, London: Fontana Press.

Evans, P, 1992, 'The State as Problem and Solution: Predation, Embedded Autonomy and Structural Change', in S Haggard and R Kaufman, eds., *The Politics of Economic Adjustment*, Princeton, NJ: Princeton University Press.

———— 1995, *Embedded Autonomy: States and Industrial Transformation*, Princeton, NJ: Princeton University Press.

———— ed, 1996, Development Strategies Across the Public–Private Divide, *World Development*, 24:6.

———— 1996a, 'Government Action, Social Capital and Development: Reviewing the Evidence on Synergy' in Evans 1996, pp. 1119–32.

———— 2000, 'Ecologies of Local Political Actors and the Struggle for Livability in Third World Cities', Paper presented at the International Conference on Democratic Decentralization, Thiruvananthapuram, May 23–27.

Ferguson, J, 1990, *The Anti-Politics Machine: 'Development', Depoliticization and Bureaucratic Power in Lesotho*, Cambridge and New York: Cambridge University Press; reissued in 1994: Minneapolis and London: University of Minnesota Press.

Fine, B, 2001, *Social Capital versus Social theory: Political Economy and Social Science at the Turn of the Millennium*, London and New York: Routledge.

Fiorina, M and Skocpol, T, eds., 1999, *Civic Engagement in American Democracy*, Washington, DC: Brookings Institute Press.

Foley, M and Edwards, B, 1999, 'Is It Time to Disinvest in Social Capital?', *Journal of Public Policy*, 19:2, pp, 141–73.

Goldberg, E, 1996, 'Thinking About How Democracy Works', *Politics and Society*, 24:1, pp. 7–18.

Gordon, D M, Edwards, R and Reich, M, 1982, *Segmented Work, Divided Workers: the historical transformation of Labour in the United States*, Cambridge: Cambridge University Press.

Granovetter, M, 1973, 'The Strength of Weak Ties', *American Journal of Sociology*, 78:6, pp. 1360–80.

—— 1985, 'Economic Action and Social Structure: The Problem of Embeddedness', *American Journal of Sociology*, 91:3, pp. 481–510.

Grootaert, C, 1997, 'Social Capital: "The Missing Link"', in *Expanding the Measure of Wealth: Indicators of Environmentally Sustainable Development*, Washington DC: World Bank.

Harrison, L and Huntington, S P, 2000, *Culture Matters: How Values Shape Human Progress*, New York: Basic Books.

Harriss, J, 1977, 'Problems of Water Management in Hambantota District' in B H Farmer, ed., *Green Revolution?*, London: Macmillan.

Harriss, J, Kannan, K P and Rodgers, G, 1990, *Urban Labour Market Structure and Job Access in India: A Study of Coimbatore*, Geneva: International Institute of Labour Studies (Research Series no. 92).

Harriss, J and P, de Renzio, P, 1997, '"Missing Link" or Analytically Missing?: The Concept of Social Capital, An Introductory Bibliographic Essay', *Journal of International Development*, 9:7, pp. 919–37.

Hart, K, 1988, 'Kinship, Contract, and Trust: The Economic Organization of Migrants in an African City Slum', in D Gambetta, ed., *Trust: Making and Breaking Cooperative Relations*, Oxford: Basil Blackwell, pp. 176–93.

Heller, P, 1996, 'Social Capital as a Product of Class Mobilization and State Intervention: Industrial Workers in Kerala, India', *World Development*, 24:6, pp. 1055–72.

—— 1999, *The Labour of Development: Workers and the Transformation of Capitalism in Kerala, India*, Ithaca and London: Cornell University Press, 1999.

Hodgson, G and Rothman, H, 1999, 'The Editors and Authors of Economics Journals: A Case of Institutional Monopoly?', *Economic Journal*, 109:453, pp. 165–86.

Isaac, TM Thomas with Richard W Franke, 2000, *Local Democracy and Development: People's Campaign for Decentralized Planning in Kerala*, Delhi: LeftWord.

Jacobs, J, 1961, *Death and Life of Great American Cities*, New York: Random House (and later editions).

Jayaraman, R and Landjouw, P, 1999, 'The Evolution of Poverty and Inequality in Indian Villages', *World Bank Research Observer*, 14:1, pp. 1–30.

Jeffrey, C and Lerche, J, 2000, 'Dimensions of Dominance: Class and State in Uttar Pradesh' in C J Fuller and V Benei, eds., *The Everyday State and Society in Modern India*, New Delhi: Social Science Press.

Keane, J, 1998, *Civil Society: Old Images, New Visions*, Cambridge: Polity Press.

Krishna, A, and Uphoff, N, 1999, 'Mapping and Measuring Social Capital: A Conceptual and Empirical Study of Collective Action for Conserving and Developing Watersheds in Rajasthan, India', World Bank Social Capital Initiative, Working Paper no. 13.

Kumar, S and Corbridge, S, 2001, 'Programmed To Fail? Development Projects and the Politics of Participation', mimeo, Department of Geography, University of Cambridge.

Lal, D, 1983, *The Poverty of 'Development Economics'*, London: Institute of Economic Affairs (Hobart Paperback no. 16).

Lemann, N, 1996, 'Kicking in Groups', *The Atlantic Monthly*, 277, April 1996, pp. 22–6.

Levi, M, 1996, 'Social and Unsocial Capital: A Review Essay of Robert Putnam's *Making Democracy Work*, *Politics and Society*, 24:1, pp. 45–55.

Mayer, P, 2000, '"An Italy of Asiatic Dimensions": What 19th Century Italy Can Tell Us About India in the 21st Century', Seminar Paper, Department of Politics, University of Adelaide; see also the revised version of this paper, published as 'Human Development and Civic Community in India: Making Democracy Perform', *Economic and Political Weekly*, 36:8.

Moore, M, 1994, 'How Difficult is it to Construct Market Relations? A Commentary on Platteau', *Journal of Development Studies*, 30:4, pp. 818–30.

Moore, M and Putzel, J, 1999, *Thinking Strategically About Politics and Poverty*, Working Paper no. 101, Institute of Development Studies, University of Sussex.

Morrow, V, 1999, 'Conceptualizing Social Capital in Relation to the Well-Being of Children and Young People', *Sociological Review*, 47:4, pp. 744–65.

Moser, C, 1996, *Confronting Crisis: A Comparative Study of Household Responses to Poverty and Vulnerability in Four Urban Communities*, Environmentally Sustainable Development Studies and Monograph Series no. 8, Washington, DC: World Bank.

Mosley, P, Harrigan, J, and Toye, J, 1991, *Aid and Power*, 2 vols., London: Routledge.

Mosse, D, 1994, 'Authority, Gender and Knowledge: Theoretical Reflections on the Practice of Participatory Rural Appraisal', *Development and Change*, 25, pp. 497–526.

Narayan, D, 1999, 'Bonds and Bridges: Social Capital and Poverty', World Bank Social Capital Library, Papers in Progress.

Narayan, D and Pritchett, L, 1996, 'Cents and Sociability: Household Income and Social Capital in Rural Tanzania', Environment Department and Policy Research Department, Washington, DC: World Bank.

North, D, 1990, *Institutions, Institutional Change and Economic Performance*, Cambridge: Cambridge University Press.

Olson, M, 1982, *The Rise and Decline of Nations*, New Haven: Yale University Press.

Pantoja, E, 1999, 'Exploring the Concept of Social Capital and its Relevance for Community-based Development, The Case of Coal-mining Areas in Orissa, India', World Bank Social Capital Initiative, Working Paper no. 18. See also World Bank Social Capital Initiative, Working Paper no. 3.

Pennant-Rea, R and Emmott, B, 1983, *The Pocket Economist*, London: Martin Robertson and The Economist.

Platteau, J-P, 1994, 'Behind the Market Stage Where Real Societies Exist', *Journal of Development Studies*, 30:3, pp. 533–77 (Part I); and 30:4, pp. 753–817 (Part II).

Polanyi, K, 1944, *The Great Transformation: The Political and Economic Origins of Our Times*, Boston: Beacon Press.

Portes, A and Landholt, P, 1996, 'The Downside of Social Capital', *The American Prospect*, 26, pp. 18–21.

Putnam, R, 1993, *Making Democracy Work: civic traditions in modern Italy*, Princeton, NJ: Princeton University Press.

———— 1993a, 'The Prosperous Community: Social Capital and Public Life', *The American Prospect*, 13, pp. 35–42.

———— 1995, 'Bowling Alone: America's declining social capital', *Journal of Democracy*, 6:1, pp. 65–78.

———— 1996, 'The strange disappearance of civic America', *The American Prospect*, 24, pp. 34–48.

———— 1996a, 'Robert Putnam Responds', *The American Prospect*, 25, pp. 26–8.

────── 2000, *Bowling Alone: The collapse and revival of American community*, New York: Simon and Schuster.

Putzel, J, 1997, 'Accounting for the "Dark Side" of Social Capital: Reading Robert Putnam on Democracy', *Journal of International Development*, 9:7, pp. 939–49.

Ramachandran, V K, 1996, 'On Kerala's Development Achievements', in J Dreze and A Sen, eds, *Indian Development: Selected Regional Perspectives*, Delhi: Oxford University Press.

Rotberg, R, 1999, 'Social Capital and Political Culture in Africa, America, Australasia and Europe', *Journal of Interdisciplinary History*, XXIX:3, pp. 339–56.

Rudner, D, 1994, *Caste and Capitalism in Colonial India: The Nattukottai Chettiars*, Berkeley: University of California Press.

Rudolph, L and Rudolph, S H,1987, *In Pursuit of Lakshmi: The Political Economy of the Indian State*, Chicago: University of Chicago Press.

Saberwal, S, 1996, *The Roots of Crisis: Interpreting Contemporary Indian Society*, Delhi: Oxford University Press.

Sabetti, F, 1996, 'Path Dependency and Civic Culture: Some Lessons From Italy about Interpreting Social Experiments', *Politics and Society*, 24:1, pp. 19–44.

Sirianni, C J and Friedland, L, 1995, Accessible from the website of the Civic Practices Network in the USA: www.cpn.org.

Skocpol, T, 1996, 'Unravelling From Above', *The American Prospect*, 25, pp. 20–5.

Skocpol, T, et al., n.d., 'How Americans Became Civic', Draft paper for Fiorini and Skocpol 1999.

Stokes, E, 1978, *The Peasant and the Raj*, Cambridge: Cambridge University Press.

Tarrow, S, 1967, *Peasant Communism in Southern Italy*, New Haven: Yale University Press.

────── 1994, *Power in Movements, Social Movements and Contentious Politics*, Cambridge: Cambridge University Press (2nd Edition).

────── 1996, 'Making Social Science Work Across Time and Space: A Critical Reflection on Robert Putnam's "Making Democracy Work"', *American Political Science Review*, 90:2, pp. 389–97.

Tendler, J, 1997, *Good Government in the Tropics*, Baltimore and London: John Hopkins University Press.

Wade, R, 1990, *Governing the Market: Economy Theory and the Role of Government in East Asian Industrialization*, Princeton, N J: Princeton University Press.

────── 1996, 'Japan, the World Bank, and the Art of Paradigm Maintenance: *The East Asian Miracle* in Political Perspective', *New Left Review*, 217, pp. 3–36.

Williamson, J, 1990, 'What Washington Means By Policy Reform' in J Williamson, ed., *Latin American Adjustment: How Much Has Happened?*, Washington: Institute for International Economics.

Willis, G, 2000, 'Putnam's America', *The American Prospect*, 11:16 [on-line edition, page numbers not available].

Woolcock, M, 1998, 'Social Capital and Economic Development: Toward a Theoretical Synthesis and Policy Framework', *Theory and Society*, 27:2, pp. 151–208.

———— 1999, 'Managing Risks, Shocks and Opportunity in Developing Economies: The Role of Social Capital', Washington, DC: World Bank (unpublished paper available through the Social Capital website).

World Bank, 1992, *Governance and Development*, Washington, DC: World Bank.

———— 1997, *World Development Report 1997/98*, Washington, DC: World Bank.

———— 2000, *World Development Report 2000/2001*, Washington, DC: World Bank.

Index